A VOICE
FROM THE PIT

"The rest may reason and welcome; 'tis we musicians know."
Robert Browning

A VOICE FROM THE PIT

Reminiscences of an Orchestral Musician

RICHARD TEMPLE SAVAGE

Bass Clarinet London Philharmonic Orchestra 1934–46
Librarian London Philharmonic Orchestra 1939–46
Bass Clarinet Royal Opera House Orchestra 1946–63
Librarian Royal Opera House 1946–82

David & Charles
Newton Abbot   London   North Pomfret (Vt)

TO MY GHOST – MY WIFE

British Library in Cataloguing Publication Data

Savage, Richard Temple, *1909*
    A voice from the pit:
    reminiscences of an orchestral musician
    1. Orchestral music. Biographies
    I. Title
    7851.092′4

Phototypeset by Northern Phototypesetting Co Bolton
Printed in Great Britain
by Billing & Sons Ltd, Worcester
for David & Charles Publishers plc
Brunel House Newton Abbot Devon

Published in the United States of America
by David & Charles Inc
North Pomfret Vermont 05053 USA

CONTENTS

Acknowledgements   6

Part One   7
The Old Days: The London Philharmonic Orchestra and the
Royal Opera House 1925–39

Part Two   63
Touring with the London Philharmonic Orchestra 1939–46

Part Three   107
The Royal Opera House Again 1946–63

Index   175

ACKNOWLEDGEMENTS

My gratitude is due to:
The Editors of "Opera" Magazine, Rodney Milnes and the
late Harold Rosenthal for their unfailing enthusiasm and assistance.
Felix Aprahamian for assisting my memory of the London
Philharmonic Orchestra in war-time.
Andrew Lamb for helping me to end my search for a publisher.

Part One

THE OLD DAYS: THE LONDON PHILHARMONIC ORCHESTRA AND THE ROYAL OPERA HOUSE
1925–39

• 1 •

"A MUSICIAN! Where DID she meet him?" exclaimed one of my wife's more elderly and county relatives on hearing in 1947 that we were to be married – thus demonstrating not only her own fossilized pre-war social attitudes but also that times were indeed changing if that question had to be asked at all. The answer, incidentally, was of course – in a pub.

When in the early thirties Anthony Baines, the bassoonist,* Raymond Bryant, the horn player, and I joined the recently-formed London Philharmonic Orchestra we must have been among the first of the new generation of public school and university educated young players without any professional musical background. Wind players were often recruited from the military bands but there were also whole families of instrumentalists: the Brains, Aubrey and his sons Leonard and Dennis; the Drapers, Haydn, Mendelssohn and Charles, the Whittakers, the Borsdorfs†, the Fawcetts and, most famous of all the Goossens who included two conductors, Eugene father and son, as well as three instrumentalists, Leon, Marie and Sidonie. They all formed their own exclusive hierarchy but as far as ordinary society was concerned only soloists were acceptable and they had to be pianists or string players. When I called at a house in Eaton Square to give a clarinet lesson to the young heir to a baronetcy it was suggested to me quite forcibly that I should have called at the tradesmen's entrance and only the timely arrival of my pupil's grandmother, a charming lady and member of the Royal Philharmonic Society who had herself arranged for the lessons, saved my outraged dignity.

Shortly before the war, with a group of players from the LPO, I was

* Anthony Baines, author of *Woodwind Instruments and their History*.
† Borsdorft, some members of the family changed their name to Bradley in World War One.

9

detailed by Sir Thomas Beecham to play at Lady Cunard's after dinner; she was entertaining the Duke and Duchess of Westminster and von Ribbentrop, the German Ambassador. We had already played a whole concert and had nothing to eat or drink but were left wandering about while the guests finished their meal. Finally Sir Thomas learned of our plight and the butler was asked to provide some refreshment. He enterted in stately fashion, bearing one solitary bottle of Guinness for twenty players. Then we played by candlelight, which made us even hotter and thirstier, so we felt a small thrill of revenge when Lady Cunard asked in rather a gushing manner for: "That little piece of Handel I'm so fond of, Thomas," and he replied sweetly: "We've just played it, my dear."

Apart from being generally overlooked, if not actually looked down on by society, our livelihood could be very precarious. As a freelance one could make a good living as long as one never took a holiday, for if a "date" should be offered and declined one would not be asked again. Native conductors, too, really needed to have private means like Boult and Beecham and be able to hire an orchestra, or perhaps start in the organ loft and descend in due course to conduct a choral festival, like Heathcote Statham at Norwich or Herbert Sumpsion of the Three Choirs Festival. Considering the members of an orchestra like the BBC or the Royal Opera House today, with their safe contracts, good salaries, extra money from recording sessions and guaranteed holidays, or the young conductors straight from University who can hope to make a career on talent alone – one might think that those were the bad old days, and yet the great London orchestras like the London Symphony Orchestra are still working on the "session" principle and without contracts, fifty years later whereas the pre-war LPO under Beecham did in fact have contracts for its players.

Good or bad, those days were nevertheless full of fascination and a great deal of laughter; in this connection it may perhaps be supposed that by relating anecdotes of mishaps in connection with the great and famous with whom I was privileged to work I am seeking to trivialize, diminish and generally debunk them. This is not the case; it is simply that, just as it was said that no man was a hero to his valet, very few conductors are heroes to the orchestral musician. Our worm's eye view from the pit of the dazzling and charismatic figures beloved of audiences is coloured by long hours of hard work which may have been rewarding and stimulating or wearying and frustrating. It was Beecham who said that an orchestra judges a conductor in the first two minutes and after that nothing can be done to alter their opinion. The requirements are: utter professionalism, a calm approach, a totally unambiguous beat, fidelity to the composer's intentions, respect for the players and a determination to achieve with them the highest standard – always tempered with an appreciation of their technical problems and a knowledge of when to stop.

Looking back over my thirty-odd years as a playing musician, I find only five men who fulfilled for me all these requirements although there were many others for whom to play was also a pleasure and a privilege – but with some reservations. The five giants for me were: Felix Weingartner, Erich Kleiber, Rudolf Kempe, Clemens Krauss and Carlo Maria Giulini. I shall write more of them in due course but I want to start at the very beginning of my musical life and try to remember more or less in sequence – a surprisingly difficult task.

· 2 ·

YOU could say that it all began with the Holy Ghost. In the early years of this century my father, Ernest John Savage, seventh child of a wholesale grocer in Aldersgate Street and who had only escaped being christened Septimus Josiah through the desperate intercession of his elder sisters, was walking home from a Church Social when he struck up an acquaintance with a Mr. Nutbeam who enquiried as to his views on the third member of the Trinity. Their subsequent arguments led to the beginning of a long friendship and shortly after their first meeting Mr. Nutbeam, a keen amateur flautist, suggested that my father should take up the clarinet. He duly purchased an instrument and paid for a quarter's lessons; his enthusiasm proved short-lived but somehow he never disposed of the clarinet which finally came to rest in the attic of our house at 37, Spencer Road, Wimbledon.

"Uncle Nutty", as I always knew him, often came with his flute to make music with my parents who were much given to piano duets, then obtainable in vast quantities in the green Peters edition — Mozart and Haydn symphonies, Handel organ concertos, and later Bach Brandenburg concertos. I was an only child but these sessions were often augmented by my uncles Jim and Ernest on the cello, my Aunt Dollie on the fiddle and Aunt Lulu who taught my mother and myself the piano. It could well have been in sheer self-defence that when, in 1925, aged sixteen, I found my father's clarinet in the attic together with an excellent tutor I set to work with a will so that I too could make my mark on the musical evenings.

My father, a pioneer of food reform, had at that time a Health Food store in Margaret Street, and afterwards in Wigmore Street, and was temporarily prosperous enough for me to have clarinet lessons at the Wimbledon Conservatoire which had been founded by an organist and rogue called Willoughby Walmisley, a man of great charm who

12

decamped with all the takings while I was still a pupil – and was never heard of again. My first teacher was Miss Broadbelt, a blonde bespectacled lady and when she left to get married I was fortunate enough to have for a term Ralph Clark, principal clarinet of the BBC Wireless Orchestra and later second clarinet in the BBC Symphony Orchestra. He insisted that I buy an up-to-date Boehm system clarinet instead of my old high-pitch one and I began my career with the Wimbledon Symphony Orchestra – conductor Theodore Otcharkoff, a genial Russian emigré – at first attending rehearsals only as I was not good enough for the concerts. I was still at school at King's College, Wimbledon where music and drama were not much encouraged at the time. My father told me that when he asked Mr. Rogers, the Headmaster, why there was no dramatic society at the school he was told that such things "led to Vice and Debauchery." However, we did have a small school orchestra, started by the English master who was reputed to be a dangerous radical. We were not very good and never could manage more than one piece at a concert: "Rosamunde" overture or the "Valse des Fleurs" from "Casse-Noisette". I seem to remember the great BBC announcer, Alvar Liddell who was also a pupil there, playing the cello solo in "William Tell" overture – perhaps our only claim to fame.

The Wimbledon Conservatoire had collapsed and I was now travelling to Parson's Green to have lessons in a very dark house from Wilfrid Keeley, a good teacher about whom I can now remember little except that he played with the BBC Wireless Military Band. I was also involved in my own home music scene with two friends, Gerald Cluer who became a school teacher and Alan Ward, a very gifted violinist who would have made a career as a soloist if his confidence had not been totally destroyed by one of those teachers who tell a pupil they must now unlearn everything and start again: so he became conductor of the D'Oyley Carte Opera for many years and I last met him conducting "Oklahoma" in the fifties.

We called ourselves the Little Orchestra and gave Saturday concerts to our friends but I was supposed to be training for a scientific career and took Higher School Certificate in physics and chemistry. There was a heat wave on the day of the chemistry practical and the stench in the lab was overpowering. I was fumbling with the apparatus, sweating profusely, when a kind attendant passed by and murmured out of the corner of his mouth: "I wouldn't do that if I were you."

Startled, I thought again and like to believe that this is why I passed! After this all my friends went to university but, contrary as ever, I did not want to – something I now regret. My father with his connections with fringe medicine and vegetarianism sent me to train with a Mr. Collins whose theory was that of the "Triple Analysis" – blood, urine and faeces – from which apparently every disease could be diagnosed. I quite enjoyed the work but unfortunately after about a year Mr. Collins died and his assistant, Miss Bottomley, was neither interested in nor capable of training me further; also she fed me exclusively on Welsh Rarebit, so I left to work for a pound a week in my father's Health Food store. Here I sold among other things, very expensive biscuits to the Duchess of Marlborough's chauffeur for her dog, checked invoices and learned to pack a neat parcel, which last skill has stood me in good stead over the years when parcelling up music.

In the summers, of course, there were the Proms. Monday was Wagner night, Friday Beethoven; we went on Wednesday, Bach night, as it was my father's choice and he was paying. He used to insist on leaving at the interval because most of the second half consisted of vast quantities of "Boosey Ballads" to piano accompaniment. Contrary to what might be supposed these were not raucous drinking songs but simply all the popular drawing-room numbers of the day published by Boosey's who helped to finance the concerts. During this part of the programme the orchestra would repair to the "George" in Great Portland Street, christened the "Glue Pot" by Sir Henry Wood as it was so difficult to extricate the players when the time came for them to return to the platform for the finale which would be the overture to "Zampa" or "Mignon" or something equally jolly. I persuaded my father to stay once – he was deeply shocked.

Here I must wander from chronological exactitude to remember Sir Henry, no respecter of composers, who rescored a great deal of the music played at the Proms in those days. Among other gems I remember the "Song of the Rhinemaidens" arranged as an orchestral piece with three solo violins instead of three clarinets – and later I myself accompanied Elsie Suddaby in a Bach aria rescored most unsuitably for triple woodwind. The Proms were certainly not over-rehearsed then; my first wife told me that she had been engaged for a season while a student at the Academy* (the College* students were

*Royal Academy of Music.
*Royal College of Music.

not invited for some reason) and there was only one rehearsal for a week of seven concerts, the standard works never being rehearsed at all! The theory was that all the parts were so meticulously marked that rehearsals were superfluous. Years later, as librarian of the London Philharmonic Orchestra, I saw many of Sir Henry's scores and the only passages to be rehearsed were indicated once and for all, including the appropriate remarks. This only confirmed to me what I had heard long before as a student attending a Royal Philharmonic Society rehearsal. During the Trio of the Schubert Great C major symphony the double bass, Eugene Cruft, started to make some query to which Sir Henry replied, still conducting: "Can't stop here, my boy – haven't stopped here for twenty-five years!"

The Prom last nights were a shade more decorous than they are today, although the promenaders did stamp their feet in time to the Hornpipe and there was a fair number of encores. When Sir Henry began to long to get home to Chorley Wood, Lady Wood, his slippers and his cocoa he would return to take his last bow in hat and overcoat, thus indicating simply and effectively that enough was enough. Lady Wood was, of course, his secretary who changed her name by deed poll to live with him after his wife and daughter left. Considerable notice was taken then of infringements of the social niceties and the poor lady was known vulgarly to the players as "the Conc".

No one could help liking Sir Henry; he was no profound musician but he had an instinct and a flair and if it were not for him most of the British concert-goers might still not have heard of Tschaikowsky! He was a shrewd businessman; aspiring singers paid fifty pounds for the privilege of auditioning for the Proms and at any concert he conducted his own orchestrations must be used – and paid for. It was the Proms, however, that were the be-all and end-all for him, every concert being thought of as if it were a Prom.

To return to 1929, it was in this year that I paid my first visit to Covent Garden. My mother provided the funds and I bought a thirteen and ninepenny ticket in the Amphitheatre for "Der Rosenkavalier". The seat looked excellent on the plan but it was in reality so far to the side that I could only see a few square feet of stage on the O.P. side – if I stood up. And whenever I stood up my seat squeaked. Bruno Walter would generally conduct only the first performance of each opera and then hand over to Robert Heger whom I found a trifle on the dull side. The cast, however, was scintillating: Gitta Alpar as Sophie, Delia

15

Reinhardt as Octavian, Elisabeth Ohms as the Marschallin and the inimitable Richard Mayr as Baron Ochs. The Royal Opera Orchestra would consist of the cream of the profession collected just for the season – the first horn was Aubrey Brain, to my mind an even better musician than his famous son, and Walter Lear* was the bass clarinet. The great chandelier which now adorns the Crush Bar then hung in the auditorium and was left dimly alight during the first act so the members of the audience could admire each other and the "Times" fashion critic take notes. The attendants, large men in kneebreeches, brought footstools for the ladies in the stalls – what would the GLC say to such an obstruction? I remember very clearly thinking: "I should like my life's work to be in this place" although it was to be another seventeen years before my wish was fulfilled.

This was to be the first of many arduous visits to the Opera House, arriving at 5.30 or 6 a.m. and paying a shilling for a stool on which one remained for hours on end, passing the time by making friends with others in the queue. I can now only remember one elderly couple, devout Wagnerians who had christened their only son Siegfried and were determined that he should be a great tenor – but I met him some while later and he was a fiddle player. In the end I became a subscriber which entitled me to an Amphitheatre seat once a week on a Monday. The seats were always rather at the side but it was a great deal better than the gallery, not to mention the hours on the stool and I felt that I was going up in the world.

*Bass clarinet of the BBC Symphony Orchestra.

· 3 ·

WHENEVER my money would stretch to it I would also go to the Queen's Hall concerts but, strange though it may seem, it never crossed my mind that I would ever be associated with the great maestri and orchestras that I heard there. Nevertheless, things began to move very slowly in that direction. My father at this time knew Harold Craxton, father of the great oboist, who was a professor at the Royal Academy of Music with Ernest Read. Through him I was able to attend one of Ernest Read's Summer Schools of Music at Bangor and was then asked to become a founder member of his Senior Orchestra, finding myself in what I now know to be very distinguished company – Evelyn Rothwell (Lady Barbirolli) Jack Brymer, Dennis Brain, to name but a few. Dennis Brain was then only about twelve but was already playing with his almost inhuman perfection; he seemed to have none of the problems that afflict mere mortal horn players.

Ernest Read was a charming, indefatigable man and at his eightieth birthday concert many years later it was plain that almost all those destined to become players of stature had passed through his hands. He had, I remember, a passion for redheads – his wife, Helen, was one – and whenever we heard that a very talented new female student was to join us our first question was always: "Has she got red hair?" – and she usually had.

I had by now made what was to prove a very wise move and acquired my first bass clarinet through the good offices of a Mr. Tabor, a flautist who sometimes visited the Wimbledon Symphony as a soloist and who sold second-hand instruments as a side-line. I remember collecting it from a very dilapidated and cluttered room near Blackfriars Bridge and paying £10 for it. My poor mother, who as a Lowland Scot was the only member of the family who ever tried to save any money, provided the funds from the little store she kept in her

17

Crown Derby coffee pot in hopes of buying a new carpet. It was not a bad instrument but simple system and lacking the bottom semi-tone which I would need for my first public performance on the instrument – the Prelude and "Liebestod" from "Tristan" with the Stock Exchange Orchestra. I evolved a simple method of obtaining this vital note by inserting the cardboard centre of a toilet roll into the bell when required; it worked very well.

During the rehearsals Edric Cundell* suggested to me that I might like to go to Music Camp. I politely declined, a decision I have *not* lived to regret. I have always felt that Music Camps epitomize the peculiar British attitude of enthusiastic amateurism – why live in a tent and compete with wasps and hedgehogs when making music? Even in those far-off days my attitude to music was already becoming that of the professional; and at this point, in 1931, I had indeed to consider ways and means of making music my profession for my father had over-reached himself irremediably and the family finances were as unstable as it was possible for them to be. His Health Food shop had been doing well, he had a factory at Enfield where "Edgar Saxon" biscuits, nut rissoles and so on were produced according to his recipes; among his writings was a successful book on food reform, "Sensible Food for All" – but he had no business sense, no partner to handle the practical side for him and he ploughed all his profits back into the business. He decided to expand by opening a vegetarian restaurant in very expensive premises opposite Selfridges. All his creditors were willing to wait except one man who finally was able to take over the whole business and continue marketing the products under my father's name while offering him a menial job in the firm. Actual bankruptcy was avoided and my father did not throw himself off Hungerford Bridge, although he had considered it – but poverty was with us to stay.

I consulted a horn player friend in the Ernest Read Orchestra, David (known as Jim) Burdett who was already at the Royal College of Music and he thought I should try to obtain an Exhibition. He knew that the College wanted a bass clarinet, in those days they were few and far between, and he arranged an audition for me with Charles Draper. I did not like to take along my own bass clarinet, now the second one I had owned, a handsome but rather ramshackle Italian

*Director of Guildhall School of Music

one, Boehm system – so I borrowed one for the occasion from the Ernest Read Senior Orchestra. For the audition I only played a few bars of the Mozart Clarinet Concerto and a couple of scales on the bass; the instrument was what they were after so I was awarded an Exhibition giving me free tuition.

I had my foot in the first door, it was 1931 and I was already twenty-two years old.

· 4 ·

CHARLIE DRAPER did not teach me for long; he was not only professor of clarinet but also a director of the firm of Louis and Co. Woodwind Instrument Makers and, not surprisingly, all his pupils had to have Louis clarinets. I fortunately owned a pair and as they were very good instruments nobody had so far complained. Things were felt to have gone too far, however, by the parents of one student who had been told that he must buy yet another and more expensive pair of Louis clarinets instead of the pair he owned already. One can only presume that the firm's profits needed a little boost at that time but the parents complained, Charlie Draper left under a little cloud and I became a pupil of Frederick (always known to us as Jack) Thurston. I don't think he thought a great deal of my chances, in fact he once suggested that I should consider taking up the tuba, but he was a fine teacher, my luck held and he was a great help to me as I shall relate in due course. He used to confuse me greatly at first by ending a lesson with: "Goodbye, see you in Room 19". For a while I searched in vain, wondering if I could be missing an important seminar of some kind, until a more worldly-wise friend explained that Room 19 was the pub near South Kensington station where I might be allowed to buy the prof. a pint. Yet another example of the usual musician's habit of calling everything and everyone something else.

It was at the College that I first played for Beecham, though only in a rehearsal of the "Eroica" symphony. I remember a great deal of laughter, generally at somebody's expense and finally at mine. Determined to be noticed, I belted out the second clarinet part in the last movement with great ferocity. A pained expression came over Sir Thomas's face. "The second clarinet" he said in those endlessly-imitated tones, "sounds exactly like a hurdy-gurdy."

In addition to studying the clarinet and, to a very small degree, the piano I was also supposed to attend classes in Aural Training where to my horror the professor, Harold Stubbs, played a note and expected me to sing a fifth above. Now, I have never been able to pitch a note; in fact on the only occasion when I tried to sing in the bath my wife, Valerie, beat on the door and asked in all seriousness if I was in pain. So I did not attend any more classes. I did have the odd ten minutes harmony and counterpoint with Dr. Gordon Jacob, whose verdict was that I had a congenital weakness for consecutive fifths, so we spent the time discussing other matters of musical interest.

It seemed to me that everything was incredibly hidebound: Hugo Anson, a senior member of the administrative staff, confided to me that he did not consider Berlioz to be a composer worthy of study; a wind ensemble was started but my suggestion that we should play Janáček's wind suite "Mladí" to give me a chance on the bass clarinet was tepidly received by Dr Jacob; I bought the parts myself and we did play it through but never gave a performance, it was all too new. Benjamin Britten, who was a student just before me (I was a rather elderly pupil) had wanted to go to Vienna to study with Webern but was not allowed to do so. One wonders what track his genius would have followed if his wish had been granted; I must admit that in this case I am not sorry for the College's traditional approach!

My youthful arrogance undiminished, I now began to long to conduct an opera and was in a position where my hopes could quite easily be realized. As a student I was able to obtain permission from the Bursar to use the Parry Theatre in the College and instrumentalists and vocalists would, I hoped, be available in abundance. My choice was Mozart's "Il Seraglio" because I already owned a full score and it was an unusual work to do in those days when it was not in the general repertory and rarely performed in England.

I was at that time patiently and for the most part hopelessly in love with a very pretty, talented and fascinating young soprano who seemed ideal for the role of Constanza. Roy Plumley has already described Aileen Street – and indeed our whole operatic venture – in his autobiography "The Days were Longer Then". He was then what one might call the *amant en titre*, in fact he may never have realized that I was the faithful adorer to whom Aileen returned every so often for what was for her, though not for me, a spell of peace and quiet. Anyway, Aileen persuaded Roy to take the speaking part of Pasha Selim and I built and painted the sketchy scenery in his father's empty

21

chemist's shop in Kingston. I also copied all the orchestral parts and put a notice on the College board inviting anyone interested to sign. As far as I can remember only one student put his name down but as that student was Peter Pears all was well. I just had to go round and press-gang my friends in College and from the Ernest Read Senior Orchestra to help me out.

Margaret Field-Hyde agreed to be the Blonda and the Osmin was Anthony Benskin who had a magnificent bass voice but no sense of rhythm whatever. It was a nightmare as one never knew what tempo he would adopt nor how long he would keep to it. My father, who was much into amateur dramatics and once embarrassed me acutely by travelling on the Tube dressed as Apollo, with gold-powdered hair, came to give a hand with the production; Aileen was in charge of the costumes; we rehearsed in people's homes and Aileen's mother provided the finance for the lighting and a professional leader for the orchestra. I overcame the problems of the chorus by borrowing a quartet of boys from Rutledge School, Merton where I had played in the local Gilbert and Sullivan productions since my schooldays. They were, I think, very successful. An advertisement, also paid for no doubt by Aileen's mother, was placed in the "Daily Telegraph" and, as there were no charges for admission, the place was packed solid for the single performance.

There were two near-disasters (three if I include the boil poor Aileen developed on her lip just before the show.) The first was caused by the timpanist from the Ernest Read Senior Orchestra who was slightly deaf and so inclined to play rather loudly, though quite well. He miscounted in the Finale of Act I and went on playing louder and louder and in all the wrong places, causing a certain amount of alarm and despondency. The second moment of anguish came in the big duet in the last act between Aileen and Peter Pears. As often happens in Mozart, a whole passage comes round twice with a pause and a cadenza in between; as we played it for the first time I discovered that they were singing the second passage and would finish long before we did. I think I tried vainly to indicate to the orchestra to jump but I was not very experienced and it was hard to know what to do so we just went on playing and somehow finished without too much loss of face. As the Press said, we "came near enough to making a musical entertainment to justify the performance as a sporting venture."

It must have been at about this time that Aileen, who did not

22

approve of cigarettes, presented me with my first pipe. I smoked it valiantly all the way on the Tube to Camden Town where I had a rehearsal, but had to leap out in haste at Euston to find somewhere to be sick. Undeterred, I continued to smoke heavily for forty years, burning holes in my trousers, the carpets and lino, always being hailed as "l'homme à la pipe" by the great French conductor, Charles Münch and being reproached by Valerie for possibly ruining my health. After a couple of bouts of bronchitis I decided to give it up once and for all and was promptly seized with an asthmatic cough and a continous need to chew gum. There must be a moral in this somewhere.

Beecham's next visit to the College was in 1934 to conduct three performances of Delius' "A Village Romeo and Juliet" by which time I had graduated to playing bass clarinet. It was a work ideally suited to a student performance as it required a large orchestra and a vast number of small-part singers; also we could have unlimited rehearsal time. At the early rehearsals we were taught the notes by Constant Lambert, but only Beecham could shape the work satisfactorily. Delius's music is notoriously difficult to conduct, it is architecturally fragmented and can sound as if it were constantly stopping and starting; in fact I think Rudolf Kempe is the only other conductor I have played for who could achieve that overall flowing smothness. As people have perfect pitch, Sir Thomas had perfect tempo – he could seize on the tempo he wanted and reproduce it exactly whenever he needed it. "A Village Romeo and Juliet" is a very beautiful piece but rather weak dramatically and without Beecham could well have seemed merely episodic.

It is strange to think that while Delius was deeply grateful to Beecham for his unswerving admiration of his music – and without it Delius might not be so widely known today – he was not, according to Eric Fenby, always in total agreement with Beecham's renderings.

It was during the Delius rehearsals that I first came across one of "Tommy's" wayward eccentricities. After a morning session Sir Hugh Allen, the Principal, summoned one member from each section of the orchestra to attend his office after our lunch break in order to mark up the parts from the score which Sir Thomas would have prepared for us in *his* lunch hour. We duly trooped in and waited. Eventually Tommy turned up with a flushed face and under his arm the score which, having wined and dined too well, he had done absolutely nothing about. So he sent us all home. In my dealings with Sir Thomas this was not an isolated incident!

23

· 5 ·

IN THE twenties the only chamber music considered suitable for high-class music clubs was, of course, for strings. Wind music was looked upon as rather low so I felt I had made something of a breakthrough when I persuaded the Wimbledon Music Club in 1929 to listen to and enjoy the Mozart Quintet for piano and four wind. The bassoonist was Jason Lewkowitch who subsequently became the contra-bassoonist for the London Philharmonic Orchestra when Beecham formed it in 1932. The LPO bass clarinet was Edward Augarde whose father had played the instrument for Wagner in the Albert Hall in 1877 but unfortunately I never heard any stories of that occasion. By 1934 Teddy Augarde was not very happy with the amount of money he could earn with the LPO as it was on a "we pay if you play" basis and the bass clarinet repertoire of the LPO was limited, so he decided to leave to join the new BBC Empire Orchestra, formed to broadcast classical music to the far-flung dominions. There he would encounter problems of another kind as one did everything "live" then and he would have to get up at one, two or four in the morning to broadcast to the remoter spots; it was a ghastly life. Anyway, his place was to fall vacant; I was by then at the College, Jason knew I had an instrument and thought I should be considered.

When I told Jack Thurston about it he appeared to pooh-pooh the idea, still suggesting I might do better with the tuba, but he decided that I must in any case have a better instrument and took me off to Boosey and Hawkes to show me a splendid bass clarinet. It had originally been made for a Scandinavian millionaire who apparently liked to play music on Saturday nights in whatever was the equivalent of his local pub, and as he was a millionaire everyone had to listen to him. When he was going through his bass clarinet phase he ordered this instrument from Boosey and Hawkes but ultimately rejected it because it did not have an automatic speaker key. I did not want an automatic speaker key, they were considered rather vulgar anyway.

"Well, there it is," said Jack Thurston.

"I can't possibly afford it" I bleated, there not being a penny in the coffers at home.

"Never mind, I'll fix it up with the College." And he did. The College paid and I paid them back as and when I was in work. When I had sent off the final instalment to bring the total to £75 7s. 6d I was delighted to receive a postal order for five shillings – it had only been £75 2s 6d after all. I also needed a new pair of clarinets but I managed to buy those myself later for £36.

I did not have an actual audition. Jason Lewkowitch phoned me up and told me to go along to Victoria Hall in Russell Square where the LPO were rehearsing on a Saturday for a Wagner concert. I sat beside Teddy Augarde for the rehearsal, no one spoke to me and I didn't play a note. Afterwards I was interviewed by Fred Laurence, manager of the orchestra, husband of Marie Goossens, a director of Goodwin and Tabb's Hire Library and also, I believe, a composer.

"What can you tell me about yourself?" he asked. "We have this vacancy you know, but Sir Thomas is a difficult man . . ."

"Well, I've just finished playing in "A Village Romeo and Juliet" for him at College."

"If you can play Delius with Tommy, you're in." And I was.

Fred Laurence was a great man. The LPO always did the Opera Season and he had an office under the stage at Covent Garden which I was to inherit after the war. The wall was covered with phone numbers without any names, but he knew them all. When under pressure he could take swift evasive action; as you approached him with your request or problem he would turn his head away, running his hand through his hair and muttering: "Don't bother me now, don't bother me now," as he strode swiftly past in the direction of the "Nag's Head" where he liked to transact most of his business and where those in search of "dates" would have to seek him out. It had a circular bar and two exits so he could make a quick getaway if he wished to avoid you. Sometimes he would change the venue to "The Sun" and this also you had to discover at the right time.

I mentioned before that his wife was Marie Goossens, the distinguished harpist. Next to his office in the Opera House was a little den where the BBC engineers would set up their equipment if there was

25

to be a relay from the theatre. Fred would wander in and say wistfully: "I can't hear the harp very well" – so the engineers would obligingly twiddle their knobs for him and the harp would come booming out on the broadcast.

There was once an awkward moment when we were rehearsing "Tannhäuser" with Felix Weingartner in 1939. It is the harpist's nightmare and Marie must have been in difficulties. Weingartner was in a bad temper and sending for Fred, not realizing he was her husband, asked sourly: "Is this the best harpist you can get?" I feel that I can tell this story as I had a similar experience after the war, rehearsing the Mozart Requiem with Bruno Walter. It was a bitterly cold morning which can make an inadequately warmed-up instrument play very flat. Steve Trier, the other basset horn, and I were dismayed to hear the maestro mutter: "And I asked especially for *good* basset-horns!"

To return to 1934, on the day that I had a phone call from Fred Laurence to say that I was "in", I remember that I had a streaming cold and was playing in the Verdi Requiem at St Martin-in-the-Fields for Arnold Goldsborough whose concerts were well known in the thirties. His orchestra was always composed of young players so there were plenty of my College friends there to congratulate me and buy me a beer. A few days later I was thrown in at the deep end by having to play at a Sunday morning rehearsal when Teddy Augarde wanted time off – and of course it had to be Delius' "Paris" which opens with a bass clarinet solo. It seemed to go quite well but the Royal Family, as the principal woodwind were known, continued to ignore me for some time to come, with the honourable exception of the first bassoon, Jack Alexandra.

Although I was now a member of the orchestra and could earn £2 8s for a concert and one rehearsal if a bass clarinet was required, Sir Thomas was chiefly known for his performances of Mozart and other classics so there were not many opportunities for bass clarinet except with a visiting conductor. A concert with the Royal Philharmonic Society generally meant an extra rehearsal at 15/-, and the Courtauld-Sargent concerts, often conducted by Malcolm Sargent himself, were on Mondays and repeated on Tuesdays, which also meant an extra rehearsal – but all this did not add up to a living wage so I had to look about me and was lucky enough to get into a small ensemble at the Old

26

Vic, playing for the theatre shows.

The first show was Shaw's "Saint Joan" with music composed by Herbert Menges who did most of the West End theatre music at that time. The conductor was Arliss Marriott who also played the flute and had apparently already invented a plan for a sort of computerized flute where everything would be electronically controlled! Besides flute and clarinet the band consisted of violin (John Stratton†) bassoon, (Cecil James‡) trombone, (Morris Smith§) possibly a cello and a trumpet for fanfares. The Saint Joan was Helen Hayes, Cecil Trouncer the Grand Inquisitor – I shall never forget his wonderful voice in that tremendously long speech in the Trial Scene – and Alec Clunes was Gilles de Rais. Shaw was present at the later rehearsals, sitting in the stalls and making comments in his beautiful soft Irish voice. I remember he was very pleased with Helen Hayes but told her that she must not try to act too much – "be simple".

The second show was "Othello" with Abraham Sofaer and Maurice Browne as Iago. The band was slightly larger then and my friend Wilfred Hambleton, later bass clarinet with the Philharmonia, joined us. Shakespeare was generally well expurgated then but on Saturday nights they put the rude bits back. During the long spells of inaction for us we played endless games of Newmarket under the stage and Ben Ashby, the other trombone* always won. One night I won and we did not seem to play after that.

The Old Vic transferred to Sadlers Wells every fortnight and the opera came to the Old Vic; it was quite dicey remembering which theatre one was supposed to be at. Another problem arose from Lilian Baylis's habit of turning up every so often to watch a Saturday matinee. She liked to get home early and the show would be put forward fifteen minutes to allow for this. Strolling down to the theatre from Waterloo one Saturday afternoon, two of us were horrified to discover that the show had already started. We had to come half an hour early every afterwards in case Miss Baylis should decide to pay us another visit.

My next job was playing for Variety at the Coliseum – twice nightly and three times on Saturdays. There was half an hour between the

*Later leader of the LSO
†Later of LSO
‡Orchestral Manager, Covent Garden after the War.
§Later of LSO

matinee and the first evening show and ten minutes between the two evening performances. By the end of Saturday night you didn't know if you were coming or going. In fact I once sent a deputy as I had another date, a colleague from the LPO and respected member of the profession but quite unused to twice-nightly, especially with long spells of idleness every so often; I am sorry to say he spent so much time refreshing himself that he was not at his best by the second show and I was asked not to send him again.

Dennis Stoll, son of Sir Oswald Stoll, had pretensions to be a conductor and had persuaded his father to let him put on this "Televariety" – TV was then just starting – a show with rather highbrow leanings. He insisted on a full symphony orchestra and most of the players were from the College or the Academy. The first oboe was Edwin Selwyn (later first oboe of the BBC Symphony Orchestra) and the second bassoon, Vernon Elliott, was contra-bassoon at Covent Garden after the war, but the first bassoon, who rejoiced in the wonderful name of Zizzolfo, was quite dreadful and made the most terrifying noise, as many bassoons did in those days, no one can imagine what it was like.

We got £7 10s a week which was very good money. The music used to accompany the acts would be taken from works like Holst's "Beni-Mora" suite or Chabrier's "España" and we had a grand ballet to the first movement of the Tschaikowsky Piano Concerto with Cyril Smith – or his wife, Phyllis Sellick – as the soloist on the stage and Leon Goossen's wife as the principal dancer.

The act I enjoyed most was Gillie Potter's monologue; I used to laugh loudly and as the audiences were terrible – twenty-five was the worst, I think he came to rely on me and if I was reading or doing the crossword and failed to laugh he would come over and look at me reproachfully.

Then there were the Ben-Bee-Hee Arabs, a trapeze and tumbling act and a French comic; of course they all brought their little signature tunes with them which we had to play. In particular there was a terrible American so-called comic whose act included an imitation of a clarinet tuning up in what he called the "ortch-tch-tchestra". I was given a little piece of paper with a phrase I had to play, he would imitate it, I would play it backwards and he would make some crack. After about a week I got very bored and tried to improve on it by playing an extended variation; to my surprise he was completely

28

thrown off balance and "dried". I was sent for by the Management and nearly lost the job.

Film sessions were also a good source of income but you had to be on the books of the fixers for the film studios. In 1934 I only got one session by chance because one of the fixers, Adolf Borsdorf, came to play at the Old Vic while I was there. It was "Lorna Doone" at Ealing, a very long day from 8 a.m. to 9.30 p.m. perpetually playing the music for the storm scene over and over again, with constant comings and goings by the big shots who had other dates and were sending deputies for part of the time. K. Ernest Irving was apt to throw a temperament and say everyone was sacked, but you just went and sat in the canteen until it blew over. On the other hand he was very good at getting money for the players, writing in two notes for a bass clarinet if you were on clarinet so that you got doubling money and spinning it all out for several sessions when it could have been done in one. All in all, although it was good money it was rather wearisome and I was not too worried not to be one of those who were in the charmed circle. I was looking forward to spring 1935 and the prospect of six to eight weeks opera season at a steady minimum of £12 a week, followed by an extended ballet season at 29/- a performance. Our salary covered performances from Monday to Friday, Saturdays were given over to rehearsals and counted as overtime; as we often had two and sometimes even three rehearsals on one Saturday there was to be one magnificent week when I would clock up a total of £21.

· 6 ·

AFTER a quick tour of Birmingham, Newcastle, Glasgow and Dundee
with Beecham, one night in each place staying in the best hotels, we
came back to London overnight and straight into the Opera House for
"Tristan" and "Lohengrin". We had started rehearsing in Dundee; I
had left the parts at home and had to telegraph my mother urgently to
send them on for me; they arrived in time – I doubt if they would now.

Frieda Leider was the Isolde and, although I do not remember any
particular excitement in that year's "Tristan", one would hear many a
fascinating tale of past rivalries and hate between the prime donne.
Charles Moor, the stage manager who also produced everything, told
a story that particularly appealed to me. It appears that there had been
on one occasion an especially deadly dispute between Frieda Leider
and the artist singing the part of Brangäne, her confidante; this had
culminated in the last act when Leider as Isolde, prostrate over the
corpse of Tristan, was about to rise to begin the "Liebestod". The
Brangäne placed her foot firmly on Isolde's train – and kept it there, so
the poor woman had to sing the whole thing more or less flat on her
face.

We opened the season with "Lohengrin" which was very eventful.
We spent the early rehearsals littering the pit with paper as we tore out
all the cuts, Beecham having decided to do the massive work complete.
As the rehearsals progressed it became obvious that the principals,
Lotte Lehmann and Lauritz Melchior, had never learned the cut
sections and did not intend to do so now. On the opening night there
were some notable silences from the stage and when we arrived back
after the second interval we knew that Sir Thomas had admitted defeat
– the parts had all been removed for the cuts to be restored. The
trouble was that when he came briskly into the pit and gave the signal
to start the Prelude to Act III we still had no music. We did our best

until the middle section where the harmonies start to get more complicated and there were one or two curious approximations. I am glad to say that during the remainder of the Prelude the parts began to reappear and be handed round – and everyone was relieved to find that the traditional large cut in Act III was back again.

Sir Thomas's grand seigneurial habit of expecting his wishes to be complied with instantly, without considering the time necessary to effect this, gave rise to many a comic situation. During the rehearsals of this same production there was another unforgettable moment. Elsa and Lohengrin were entering the cathedral for their wedding at the end of Act II – and the organ failed to come in. The instrument, I must explain, was situated high up at the side of the stage and reached by a perilous ladder.

"Who is playing the organ?"

"Felix White, Sir Thomas."

"Send him to me."

A gentle little man finally appeared.

"What seems to be the trouble, Mr. White?"

"Well, it's rather a long way up the ladder, Sir Thomas, and I'm afraid I didn't allow myself enough time."

"I see. Very well, we'll start again." But, of course, Beecham didn't allow enough time either and once again the organ missed the entry.

"What has happened this time?"

"I'm afraid he's fallen off the ladder, Sir Thomas." And indeed the poor man had, it was a very hazardous climb and he had by now quite lost his nerve.

"Oh dear – well" Beecham looked hopefully at us, "can anyone here play the organ?"

The third trombone, Bill Coleman, rashly raised his hand.

"All right, Mr. Coleman, off you go."

Bill Coleman was considerably more agile a climber than Felix White and this time the organ came in, but Sir Thomas still looked bewildered and tapped his desk, so we ground to a halt once more.

"Where on earth," he enquiried plaintively," is the third trombone?" and was greeted with shouts of delighted laughter in which, after a moment's astonishment, he joined us.

As a very new boy, "Lohengrin" was causing personal problems for me, as well; in the second act I had to play a passage in octaves with the first oboe, Leon Goossens, and found myself unable to get in tune – I was always flat. I confided my troubles to the second oboe, Horace Halstead, to whom I am eternally indebted.

"It's like this, Dick," he said, wheezing and puffing his pipe, "When Lee gets a solo he pushes the reed well in to make himself sharp so he'll be sure to stick out from the rest." So off I went to see Mr. Quilter at Boosey and Hawkes and have a bit cut off the crook of the bass clarinet so I could play sharper too.

"All those years playing second has taught me a thing or two," said Horace with a chuckle. "Composers should never write for two oboes playing in octaves; it makes it almost impossible for the second to stay in tune with one of these prima donna first oboes."

I was also learning a thing or two, playing in "La Bohème" for the first Italian conductor I had met, Vincenzo Belleza. He wore the largest number of sweaters I have ever seen at one time on one man and was constantly peeling them off or struggling into them again; but the problem was that he followed the habit of Italian maestri at that time and did not conduct *at all* in any passages of the opera where the orchestra was not actually playing. In the first act of "Bohème" particularly where there is a great deal of gambolling about and unaccompanied singing by the students, I was totally lost and never knew when to come in again.

This was also the year of what the Press headlined as the "Grace Moore Riots". The beautiful blonde film star of "One Night of Love" came to sing Mimi and although many voices as good or better, and certainly larger, could have been heard in any season, the public went wild at the idea of seeing a real live film star and the queue for the non-bookable galley seats wound all round the theatre and into the market. After queuing literally all over the weekend some of the fans would leave the head of the queue now and then for refreshments or to answer the call of nature and their places, carefully staked out with stools and cushions, would be seized by marauding bands of late but equally fanatical arrivals. The rightful claimants would return and real fist fights ensued until the police issued in force from Bow Street to restore order.

For my own choice, I would far rather have fought in 1935 to see and hear Conchita Supervia, the brilliant Spanish mezzo soprano who sang "Italiana in Algeri" and "Cenerentola." I did only one rehearsal with her, at Drury Lane, as a substitute for someone, but I went up in the lift with her. She was quite incredibly pretty with blazing blue eyes,

32

Titian hair and a tremendous personality. I staggered out of the lift and went at once to book tickets for both operas. I remember she was accompanied everywhere by her little dog, even bringing him on stage in "Italiana" which, of course, won the hearts of the British public immediately. She also sang "Carmen" with Beecham and I imagined it would be superb, I could not get to see it, – but the reviews were cool and I think comedy must have been her great forte. Tragically, she died soon afterwards in childbirth, still in her early thirties.

When it came to "Prince Igor" in that first season, Beecham was not at all happy with the chorus and in fact compared them unfavourably to a suburban church choir; he then sent for an actual church choir to replace them, from the Russian Orthodox Church in Paris. They arrived next morning but also made a poor showing at first, complaining that they had not had time for any breakfast. Provisions had to be found for them and we had to break the rehearsal.

"Breakfast!" said Beecham with scorn. "Nobody eats breakfast, surely? Do you eat breakfast?" he asked the orchestra.

"Yes, we certainly do," we assured him.

"The only possible breakfast" he assured us "is Black Velvet (Guinness and Champagne)" and this he suddenly decided to order for everyone although Maurice Johnston*, his secretary, was heard to whisper loudly "And who's going to pay?" I was careful to stick to champagne only but some of the teetotallers in the orchestra were considerably affected. The rehearsal went very well after that and it is one of my happiest memories of my first season.

*Later Musical Director of BBC, Manchester

33

DURING the 1935 summer ballet season with Colonel de Basil's Ballets Russes de Monte Carlo we left for a two-day concert visit to Brussels, ostensibly to promote British music at the International Exhibition. It was wonderful weather and Sir Thomas was sporting his straw boater; after a good dinner in the Hotel Metropole we all assembled happily in the Salle des Beaux Arts for the concert, only to discover that for some now long-forgotten reason the music appeared to have been impounded by the customs and only our instruments had so far arrived. Quite undaunted, "Tommy" quickly procured the "Meistersinger" Overture and the G minor Symphony of Mozart from a local Library and, without any preliminary announcement, this ad hoc programme was given to a bemused audience. After the interval the music must have arrived because I remember playing the overture to Ethel Smyth's "The Wreckers" which was on the original programme. However, the whole affair seemed to have had an adverse effect on Beecham for at the second concert, in spite of having all the correct music and an international broadcast scheduled and advertised, he decided to play a totally different programme again. Astonished listeners in England, including my own family, kept hearing one piece announced and a different one played throughout the broadcast and the poor fourth flute, who had come all the way just to play in Arnold Bax's "Garden of Fand", which was never performed, had nothing to do but get dreadfully drunk.

Next day we travelled back by boat and train in time to go straight into the theatre for "Firebird" in the evening and then I returned to Wimbledon where I was still living with my parents; but at twenty-six I was finding it all rather irksome. The situation with Aileen would obviously never be resolved in my favour – in fact, in the following year she married Frank Rendall, a handsome baritone who had sung

34

the Second Peasant in "A Village Romeo and Juliet" at College. I needed peace and a place of my own. I had been friendly for some time with Hilda Parry, a young fiddle player I had met in the Ernest Read Senior Orchestra and who subsequently joined the Kathleen Riddick Orchestra. She was good fun, a good musician and we shared a fondness for cats. We got married in the early autumn at Kingston Registry Office, leaving a note for my parents who were justly incensed; and I had to go up to play in "Un Ballo in Maschera" as the second clarinet was ill. I had to sight-read the whole opera.

I had made the break from home but unfortunately the marriage was a total disaster and we eventually went our separate ways. Hilda was later very conscious of the fact that she should never have married anyone at all and when, ten years later, I had the opportunity of making a happy and lasting marriage she did all she could to make the divorce easy for me, even to the extent of secretly paying a large proportion of the costs. We lived at first in a flat in Wimbledon where we owned, rather rashly, two female cats, Bit and Wink, who both managed to give birth while we were on holiday in Cornwall and I received an irate telegram from my father who was now minding eleven cats instead of two. After finding homes for the kittens, we moved with the original two cats to a flat in a lovely situation in Highgate which, for the large sum of six pounds a week, we kept until the outbreak of war.

From September 23rd to October 5th 1935 it was the short Imperial League of Opera season; Beecham, Clarence Raybould and Albert Coates conducted. Clarence Raybould, Sir Adrian Boult's assistant at the BBC, was a very professional and generally good-natured conductor but during his rehearsals of "Bohème" he became increasingly exasperated by Beecham's perpetual back-seat driving from the stalls until he finally put down his baton, turned round and protested: "Sir Thomas, I really must ask you to allow me to conduct the opera in my own way."

"But of course, my dear boy, you must do what you like," came the amiable reply. "Just as long as you do it *my* way." After that we were all, of course, on Clarence Raybould's side.

Albert Coates, a fine conductor originally trained in Russia, did the "Siegfried". This was the only time I played for him in opera but I remember him in his later years as no respecter of the composer's intentions as to tempi – he would put rubati in the "Casse-Noisette"

Suite and in Beethoven's Pastoral that had to be heard to be believed. I also played the basset-horn obbligato to the aria "Non piu di fiori" from "La Clemenza di Tito" at a pre-war Sunday concert at the Opera House when he was conducting and his wife* was singing. He put the whole aria down a semi-tone which made it virtually unplayable though I did my best. In 1935 the cuts he put in "Siegfried", when we went on tour to Brimingham a week later with a small orchestra, were staggering. It was quite usual for Wagner to be heavily cut but this was "Cut eight bars, play eight bars" all over the place; it worked but made it very difficult for us.

Naturally it was Beecham who conducted Delius' "Koanga". It was a first performance and he was anxious and bad-tempered throughout rehearsals; ever afterwards if he seemed at all liverish the word would go round that he was in a "Koanga mood". The producer was as usual Charlie Moor whose motto was "when in doubt do nothing" so the Voodoo scene was a pitch-dark, apparently empty stage. When Beecham enquired: "Is anything going to happen, Mr. Moor?" he was told that it would be all right on the night. I can't recall that it was much better. The heroine, Oda Slobodskaya, was immensely tall and when she appeared at the dress rehearsal not only "blacked up" but wearing a comical high headdress Beecham became convulsed with laughter and asked her if she really intended to come on like that at the performance. She became very angry in a heavy Russian accent and ended by throwing her shoe at him which fortunately seemed to amuse him even more and greatly improve his temper. To crown it all we had two banjo players who sat just in front of the conductor's desk and squabbled ceaselessly. It transpired that Fred Laurence had engaged them without realizing that they were deadly enemies. Once they disappeared altogether and when Sir Thomas enquired after the "exotic gentlemen", as he liked to call them, he had to be told that they were outside having a fight. Not surprisingly, by the time we got to Birmingham on tour he had dispensed with them.

After Birmingham another orchestra took over and we returned to London for the winter concert season. I had been thinking for some time that I ought to acquire a basset horn as I should certainly need one if Strauss's "Der Rosenkavalier" came into the repertory, so I went once more to Boosey and Hawkes and asked Mr. Quilter to keep his

*Vera de Villiers

36

eyes open for one. Sure enough, shortly afterwards a man came into the shop with a bundle containing an instrument he could not identify and which had been given to him in a settlement of a debt. It turned out to be a beautiful Buffet basset-horn in shocking condition. He wanted £15 for it and I had another £15 worth of work done on it and was ready when "Rosenkavalier" duly turned up in the spring of 1936.

It was about this time that I experienced my first recording sessions at the EMI studios in Abbey Road, St. John's Wood. We would all huddle on to a replica of the Queen's Hall platform with, for some reason known only to Beecham, the oboes placed in front of the flutes, clearing our throats as hard as we could and praying that we would not get an irresistible tickle once the red light was on. The engineers were absolutely paranoid about extraneous noises and at my first session, recording the Prelude and Closing Scene from "Koanga", the problem seemed almost insurmountable as in the middle of the playing time of four minutes we all had to turn over with loud rustles to start the second extract. Beecham's suggestion that the microphones should be switched off for a few seconds and then switched on again was at first viewed as highly unorthodox, but that was what had to be done. The whole orchestra turned over the pages as one man and seized the opportunity for a quick cough as well.

On one occasion the engineers were driven quite desperate by a faint, persistent clicking noise which they could not manage to locate. After prowling round the studio for a long time with their microphones, glaring at us accusingly and making us all feel guilty, they finally traced it to the timpani player's false teeth. Jimmy Bradshaw was not only a very brilliant player – to watch him bring up a crescendo roll was a great experience – but a very conscientious one who counted every bar's rest meticulously and his dentures clicked softly as he mouthed the numbers. He was very insulted, poor man, but was finally persuaded to limit himself to counting the bars in his head.

I was always fascinated by those direct recordings on to wax and later, as Librarian of the LPO, I was able to attend several sessions in the actual recording room at the invitation of Walter Legge, Director of EMI. I still remember with pleasure the hot, sweetish smell of the wax and the wonderful simplicity of the method by which the turntable was kept at a constant speed – a weight and pulley similar to the mechanism of a grandfather clock; gravity being constant there could be no problems caused by any fluctuation in speed. On the other hand, when we made the much-publicized recording of "Petrouchka" with Ernest Ansermet for Decca at the end of the war, electrical power was used to spin the turntable and it turned out that there had been variations in current (very common at that time) causing the speed and consequently the pitch to vary from record to record. The entire set had to be made again. One disc would be cut with a diamond stylus and then played back to check the balance and so on. Unfortunately, after being played back it was of no further use and had to be sent to be melted down so the process would be repeated until they felt that they might print from the next one. It used to seem to me that if they had recorded two discs at the same time they would have one left to print if it should prove satisfactory, instead of destroying the only one available. After a while they did in fact do this; so I imagine that the high cost of the equipment in the early days had something to do with it.

Arthur Clarke, the chief recording engineer, was a delightful, rather taciturn man who rarely showed emotion but there were two situations in which he was liable to turn the air blue with his wrath. The wax cut from the disc by the stylus was drawn away by a powerful suction into a tube just by the needle but occasionally this thread of wax would break or take the wrong turning and curl itself round the needle, causing a loud screaming noise and the total destruction of that particular disc. The second possible disaster could be caused by a stylus striking a small imperfection in the wax and splitting in half. "Sorry – bad wax!" would come the call and once again everything had been ruined.

I also met a very interesting member of the technical back-room boys who had become totally bald at a very early age; he had the very delicate task of closing up the gaps in the King's Christmas broadcast caused by George VI's speech hesitation, before it was sent out again in the evening to the far corners of the Empire. In three or four hours, with no easy tapes to cut and splice but endless recording and re-recording, he would remove all the awkward pauses – a really masterly job. It must have been nerve-racking too, I am not surprised that he lost all his hair.

Most of the recordings I made in the early days were with Beecham but I once had to play for Sir Hamilton Harty in the Bax "Picaresque Comedy Overture". We did it all in one session; I was still a very new boy and discovered to my horror that I suddenly had several bars all on my own. On hearing the play-black Sir Hamilton commented in his gentle Irish voice that the bass clarinet seemed to have had "rather a bumpy ride". This was one occasion when I was devoutly thankful to know that the wax would now be destroyed, obliterating my shame while I concentrated on getting it right next time.

· 8 ·

THE LPO played for various festivals before the war and I particularly enjoyed the one in Norwich in the summer of 1936. The town is delightful, the weather was good and with various concerts at different times and places throughout the day the atmosphere was sociable and pleasant. I stayed at the Maid's Head; Scott Goddard of the "Morning Post" was there and Astra Desmond, one of the most musically intelligent of the oratorio singers of her day. She was the soloist in the first performance of Vaughan Williams' "Five Tudor Portraits", conducted by Heathcote Statham. The words are by the Elizabethan poet, Thomas Skelton, and it is strange to think that some of them were considered rather too racy both by the choir and the audience. The other notable first performance was of Benjamin Britten's "Our Hunting Fathers" and Auden's verses attacking blood sports also surprised the Festival audience not a little. It was conducted by the composer and I understand that Sophie Wyss, the singer, recounts in her memoirs that the orchestra behaved so badly at rehearsals we had to be reproved by Vaughan Williams! I confess I have no recollection of this although we certainly had problems. At this time Britten was very young, full of brilliant new ideas but quite unused to relating to hardened orchestral players. The work was full of difficult technical tricks and the orchestra was more or less in revolt at being asked to attempt them. There were acrid exchanges like this:

Player. This glissando is just impossible.
Britten. There's a man in Chicago who can play it.
Player. Well, you'd better get him to do it, then.

In the end, what we couldn't manage we left out. I have no doubt that modern players would wonder what we found so difficult.

Beecham conducted Delius' "Mass of Life" which meant that we had to send for a certain Captain Waterhouse who played the bass oboe. He was a total mystery to me, I never knew his first name – he was always referred to simply as Captain Waterhouse – I never talked to him; he would appear, tallish, faintly military, not young, and vanish again. I often wondered what he did during those long, long spells when he was not playing the bass oboe, an instrument for which opportunities of employment were very rare indeed. But I never discovered.

We also performed the Bach "Magnificat" with Leon Goossens playing the obbligato on the oboe d'amore but when we went to Sheffield Festival Henry Wood was in charge and rescored it all for a sort of Straussian orchestra, which was bad enough, but he also cut out the oboe d'amore and had it all played on the oboe so Leon did not get his extra fee. This is the kind of thing that is never popular. Sir Henry was in a bad mood generally; we were Beecham's orchestra so he did not want us in the first place and also Paul Beard had just left us to go to the BBC; Sir Henry seemed to feel he should not have done so just when were contracted to play for him at Sheffield, so he showed his displeasure by being very cool towards our new leader, David McCallum, who could hardly be said to be to blame for anything.

The highlight of the Sheffield Festival was seeing and hearing Rachmaninoff. We performed his cantata "The Bells" though nobody quite seemed to know why he did not in the end conduct it himself, and I was sitting close to him as he played his Second Piano Concerto. He wore an evening dress that was literally green with age, sat very still and hummed throughout on one note while, without any histrionics, he produced the most beautiful playing I have ever heard – an absolute revelation.

The only memory I have of Leeds Festival is of a work by Lennox Berkeley – "Jonah", I think, – with a large section for unaccompanied voices. The choir were wavering about more and more until by the end of the rehearsal the only person still in tune was the soloist, Parry Jones, who had perfect pitch. Finally a few horns were cued in from time to time to keep everyone in tune.

As the winter season approached I would pick up all the available prospectuses from Queen's Hall to see how many works would need a bass clarinet. In addition to the Courtauld-Sargent and Royal Philharmonic Society concerts which I mentioned earlier, there were regular Sunday afternoon concerts by Beecham and from time to time

we played for the Royal Choral Society as well. Also there were
Harold Holt Celebrity Concerts with stars like Kreisler or Caruso and
sometimes we were delivered up as a sacrifice into the hands of
aspiring conductors who could afford to hire us and try out their
technique. We really plumbed the depths with one Polish gentleman
who must have been extremely wealthy as there could be no other
possible reason for allowing him on to the podium; luckily we knew
the piece and managed in spite of him. Sydney Beer was certainly one
of the wealthy conductors, the family money came from diamonds and
later I used to take his scores to him at Claridges, but he was also a
good musician and a very nice man; unfortunately he suffered acutely
from nerves and in performance his beat would become quite
incomprehensible. He confided to me once that he was disappointed
not to be able to achieve better results. "I listen to all Toscanini's
records and do just what he does but it doesn't sound the same," he
said pathetically.

If I have not mentioned playing for Sir Adrian Boult, the kindest and
most courteous of men, it is because he remained loyal to his BBC
orchestra and did not often conduct the LPO until much later on. We
only did a couple of concerts with him, one that I remember was on the
occasion of the award of the Royal Philharmonic Society's Gold
Medal to Richard Strauss. We played "Also sprach Zarathustra" and
there was what one might call a very uncoordinated bit both at the
rehearsal and the performance but fortunately the aged composer
appeared to be fast alseep at the time. Boult was a very fine conductor
of Elgar and Vaughan Williams and in no way limited – he tackled
everything including the first performances in England of Berg's
"Wozzeck". I have to admit that, for me, much of his interpretation of
the classics seemed a trifle on the dull side. I think his remark
concerning the overture to "Figaro" perhaps explains this. This
overture is supposed to take the same time to play as it would to boil an
egg. "I like my egg well done" Boult would say – and hard-boiled eggs
are apt to be a little stodgy.

It was at a Queen's Hall Charity Concert shortly before the war that
I had my first chance to score a piece for a professional orchestra
although I had been given to trying my hand at orchestration for
family or friendly ensembles since my schooldays. Dino Borgioli was
to sing one of Liszt's Petrarch sonnets and a song by Respighi whose
title I have forgotten, and they are only written for voice and piano.

Beecham wanted to do them with orchestra and Fred Laurence gave me the job. I suppose I did get paid but I don't remember that either! I have to confess that quite a quantity of Liszt got lost in the process as the long postlude after the singer has finished would have left poor Borgioli standing on the platform doing nothing for an unconscionable time, so I had to do what was known as "browning it off"; and one observant critic remarked in his review that it sounded "somewhat truncated". I had been through the score with Sir Thomas but at the rehearsal I gave a guilty start when I heard him call for "the composer". However, when I approached the rostrum to the accompaniment of sotto voce gibes from my colleagues, all he had to say was: "Mr. Savage, we need another note."

"What note would you like, Sir Thomas?" I meekly enquired.

"I think we'll have an E flat."

So E flat it was and I retired once more to oblivion.

· 9 ·

BY THE April to June opera season of 1936 I was playing my second "Ring" with Beecham. My memories of them are as lightweight, lyrical and a trifle on the fast side; but the really unforgettable experience in 1936 was hearing Kirsten Flagstad, the supreme Brünnhilde, for the first time. The audiences cheered her to the echo and even the most hardened player in the pit knew he was hearing a unique voice. Beecham also conducted "Die Meistersinger" uncut which made a very long evening but he always said it was no use cutting that opera as it always took just as long to play. A particularly unusual and charming star of that show was the theatre cat, a stalwart tabby who used to wander down the empty, moonlit Nuremberg street at the end of the second act and was always loudly applauded. I never knew if a special stage-hand pushed him on at the right moment or if he just made his way to supper by this route, but it was one of the happiest stage effects I have ever seen.

We had what you might call time and motion problems again when rehearsing the end of that same act. After the fight is over the Night Watchman walks slowly across the back of the stage from the OP side, blows his horn (this is represented by the off-stage tuba), sings a little song and blows another call before he exits on the prompt side. The tuba player has to make his way round backstage from the OP side to the prompt side to be ready for the second call. It is a long way and Bob Chator was having difficulty in negotiating the impedimenta and covering the distance in time, with the result that the Nightwatchman blew a silent note.

"He hasn't quite got there, Sir Thomas."

"Let's do it again, starting from that side to save time."

Off we went but poor Bob Chator who only knew that "they were going to do it again" was racing back to his original starting-point on

44

the OP side while the Watchman had found himself delivering another silent raspberry. Thoroughly exasperated, Sir Thomas decided to go right back to square one and the Watchman returned to make his original entrance on the OP side; but conflicting messages reached the hapless tuba player who was, as usual, en route for somewhere but never there. The concerted wrath of all those in authority fell on him and he rushed screaming from the theatre and was never seen again. I don't remember any trouble with his replacement who must have been of sterner stuff.

I knew the regular tuba player, Bill Scannell, well and liked him very much. He was a big, jolly Northerner who was noted for his magnificent solos in "Siegfried". They are very taxing and exhausting so during the "Ring" he would go into strict training – no drinking or smoking – and in consequence became very low-spirited and inclined to have rows with his colleagues. As soon as the "Ring" was over he was his usual genial self again.

Fritz Reiner came for "Rosenkavalier", "Parsifal" and "Tristan". He was a very professional but rather sour-faced conductor, gifted with a prodigious memory. As it was my first "Rosenkavalier" I was too busy getting the notes right to have much time to appreciate the performance and it was not until I played it under Erich Kleiber that I began to understand the subtleties of the score. In "Tristan" Reiner accused me of playing a wrong note, which was upsetting – particularly as I managed to hear the test record of that performance which Beecham had made (it was never issued) and discovered that I had, in fact, played correctly – but I never met Reiner again to tell him so. In "Parsifal" the second and third clarinets have a few bars solo and on one occasion Frank Hughes, the third clarinet, missed two of them. A year or two later, when the LPO was entertaining the Berlin Philharmonic Orchestra at the Savoy, players were passing up their menus to be signed by Furtwängler, Beecham and Reiner. Frank Hughes was much surprised to get his back from Reiner with the addendum "You owe me two bars!"

I was not concerned with "Les Contes d'Hoffman" that season, for which I am sorry as Beecham reputedly engaged the services of Mr. Maskelyne of Maskelyne and Devant, the illusionists, for some special effects which must have been fun. Malcolm Sargent conducted Charpentier's "Louise" which was not such fun. Opera was not his forte and it was obvious from the first rehearsal that he knew far less about the work than the experienced French principals who had come over from the Opéra Comique; but this did not deter him from telling them how it should be done.

I frankly admit that I never enjoyed playing for Sargent and if he thought of me at all it must have been as that tiresome little man who kept arguing with him and trying to catch him out. In spite of his undoubted charm he could be arrogant and condescending and had an incurable propensity for trying to teach other experts their jobs. He would tell our leader, Paul Beard, how to bow the end of the first part of the "Dream of Gerontius" – already clearly bowed by Elgar himself – or say kindly to the violas: "You play divisi here" when the short answer was "How else could we play it?"

I had a rehearsal with him of a Bach Passacaglia and Fugue, orchestrated by Respighi, just at the end of my time at College when I had already joined the LPO. "Of course, we shall get professionals for the actual concert" he told the discomfited wind section. The very next morning he came to rehearse the LPO and met me in my professional capacity. "I am very pleased with your progress, Savage" said he graciously – never at a loss.

There was not the insistence on respect for the composer's intentions that there is today and Sargent was by no means alone in interfering constantly with orchestration, (he even added four horns to the Mozart "Requiem", in which there are none) but the reasons he would give for his cosmetic treatments never seemed to me to be valid. For example: in Mendelssohn's "Ruy Blas" overture there is a scale up for all the orchestra but without trumpets which Sargent added because "of course, in Mendelssohn's day the natural trumpets could not have played the scale." However, if one turns over the page, the same passage comes again – this time with the trumpets. So Mendelsshon was not writing for natural trumpets, he just didn't want them to play the first time. Of course I pointed this out and Sargent had the grace to look embarrassed; if he had only just said: "Well, it's because I like it better this way," I could have forgiven him more easily.

After all this it will be easy to understand why we all enjoyed ourselves so much at a public rehearsal for the Royal Philharmonic Society at Queen's Hall when Sargent was rehearsing an occasional piece written for Coronation Year by Vaughan Williams, making comments on and proposing alterations to the orchestration. We were suddenly startled by a shout from the back of the hall: "Hey! What are you doing to my piece?" Unnoticed, the composer had been there all the time.

To be fair, we were very far then from the present Age of Authenticity; it was normal practice before the war to double woodwind for Beethoven and Schubert in a big hall with a big orchestra, (Mengelberg even did it for Tschaikowsky as well), and there was no hesitation in following Weingartner's suggested rescoring in his "On Conducting Beethoven" in order to make musical sense of passages where, owing to the limitations of natural horns and trumpets in Beethoven's day, the composer's intentions had not been fully realized. This applied particularly to the Fifth and Ninth Symphonies. Composers like Mozart and Haydn wrote for the capabilities of the instruments available to them, but Beethoven was thinking ahead of his time. One can realize how right it was to make some adjustments, for example: in the "Eroica" the horns literally seem to disappear in one tutti because the original natural horns could not have managed the melody and had to be given purely trivial notes. Also, in the first movement of the Fifth Symphony (bar 303, to be pedantic!) Beethoven had to write the famous opening "Victory" theme for two bassoons as in that particular key the notes simply were not on the instrument for the horns. The result tends to be comic rather than heroic and only purists continue to keep to bassoons; it is, as always, a matter of taste and judgement.

To return to Covent Garden – the opera season was the only time when I received a regular salary; in the ballet season which followed it was 29/- a performance if the bass clarinet should be needed, but I liked to play as much as possible, for the experience as well as for the cash, so I would volunteer to play second clarinet if someone wanted a ballet off in order to get home early. It was rather a slog but at least the orchestra was seated in such a way that I could catch an occasional glimpse of the stage and see Massine in his wonderful dance as the bar-tender in "Union Pacific" or the lovely Baronova, the baby ballerina of the three young stars – Riabouchinska and Danilova being the other two. There were no full-length ballets taking up an entire evening – only Act II of "Swan Lake" and "Aurora's Wedding" from "Sleeping Beauty". Two numbers from "Casse-Noisette" were interpolated, the Dance of the Sugar Plum Fairy and the Chinese Dance, so I could earn my bread and butter by playing for a total of four minutes out of the whole evening. Massine was very keen on choreographing symphonic works so we had ballets to Beethoven's Seventh, Tschaikowsky's Fifth (Les Présages) and even Brahms' Fourth (Choreateum) – about the least balletic work imaginable. We wore tails for the opera but it was black tie for the ballet; my eccentric friend, Tony Baines the bassoonist, was playing his first ballet season in 1936 and did not know about this so he turned up in tails. Without a moment's hesitation, he went in search of a bottle of black ink and dipped his white tie in it; of course it dripped all down his shirt and everywhere but he did not mind in the least.

Later on, if the ballet season had not started too well, the management had two solutions: either they would put on a half-price matinee to get the children in or they would announce a Gala evening at very inflated prices. Beecham was invited to lend lustre to one of these Galas by conducting a performance of "Tamara" by Balakireff. It was a favourite piece of his in the concert hall but naturally the dancers needed it to be taken at a fairly moderate tempo. It immediately became apparent that Sir Thomas had not the slightest intention of making any concessions, in fact I suspect he whipped us up a little more than usual and the wretched dancers were tumbling about in their efforts to keep pace. As they took their bows, gasping and streaming with sweat, their regular conductor, Effrem Kurz, could be seen peering down, ashen-faced, from a box while Tommy murmured to us with a happy smile: "That made the buggers hop!" I went down in the lift at Covent Garden station afterwards with Effrem Kurz who had still not recovered and kept staring and muttering: "It was terrible, terrible!"

· 10 ·

IN NOVEMBER 1936 the Dresden State Opera came to Covent Garden and Beecham took the LPO on a tour of Germany – Berlin, Dresden, Leipzig, Munich, Frankfurt, Mannheim and Cologne. In view of the political climate the Jewish members of the orchestra were given the chance to opt out but I do not remember any of them doing so and, in addition, Sir Thomas insisted on taking with him as his personal assistant Dr. Berta Geissmar*, a hideous and most endearing lady who was as Jewish as she could be. She had been Furtwängler's assistant and had only recently been obliged to leave Germany; her newly-acquired colloquial English was put to unexpected uses, for example, she would always address me affectionately as "Richard, you bloody fool!" It was delightful to see Berta at Beecham's side as he was greeted by all the Nazi officials on Munich station and to know that all respect would have to be paid to her as his assistant.

Someone at the big party given for us in Munich did ask me if we had many Jewish players in the orchestra but no real sense of the horrors that had already begun managed to reach us. On the other hand, there was a very large "Anti-Bolshevismus" exhibition on in Munich. Of course, there were uniforms everywhere, it was impossible to dodge the collecting boxes with "Kraft durch Freude" on them held out by brown shirts on every corner. We doggedly replied "Rule Britannia" to every "Heil Hitler" and when, in a Leipzig restaurant, everyone was expected to move to make room for a party of Hitler Youths, we sat tight; but we were very glad that we had nearly finished anyway and could soon leave without loss of face. All in all, the only really frightening moment for me was after a concert in the industrial town of Ludwigshaven, across the Rhine from Mannheim where we were

*Author of Musik im Schatten der Politik (The Baton and the Jackboot)

staying. As I finished at the interval I set out to walk back to Mannheim over the bridge. It was pitch dark and, in the tall, factory-like buildings on each side of the narrow street, strange and sinister celebrations seemed to be going on with sounds of hoarse singing and martial crashing, rather like the Gibichungs in "Götterdämmerung". The air seemed full of menace and I hurried to reach the reassuring eighteenth-century elegance of Mannheim again and to wonder why I had been so afraid.

I have little recollection of the actual concerts but I know that Beecham would have liked to include some Mendelssohn in the programme; however, diplomatic advisers dissuaded him. It would have been good to be able to play Mendelssohn in the Leipzig Gewandhaus from which the Nazis had only recently removed the composer's statue. I only played in two pieces: Lord Berners' "The Triumph of Neptune" and the Prelude and Wedding March from Rimsky-Korsakov's "Coq d'Or", so I managed to go to the opera twice – Erich Kleiber conducting "Flying Dutchman" in Berlin and a lovely production of Flotow's "Marta" in Munich. I also wandered about and tried to go into what looked like a museum but I was fiercely repelled by sentries as it turned out to be the Nazi Headquarters, the Brown House.

From a linguistic point of view we did not distinguish ourselves. In Berlin, Leon Goossens wondered why the chambermaid looked so startled when he asked for some soap for the bathroom – until she returned obediently carrying a pot of mustard. Percy Frosdick, a vegetarian fiddle player, also alarmed the waiter who was advancing upon him with a juicy steak by waving his arms and crying angrily: "Nein, nein – ich bin Gemüse!* As for me, I tried to be a little too clever and make use of my operatic German: I used a phrase culled from the libretto of "Der Rosenkavalier" (Sie sind die Güte selbst) to express my thanks when someone passed me the bread at the big Munich party – and wondered why they all fell about laughing. I suppose it must have sounded as ridiculous to them as "Sir, your most obedient . . ." or "I am eternally indebted to you." I also had a brief encounter with a very large policeman who wanted to fine me on the spot for crossing the road against the traffic lights. I managed to mumble: "Ich verstehe nicht" and he definitely called me a stupid Pole.

*No, no–I am a vegetable!

At this point I thought it would be the appropriate moment to try out the phrase: "Take me to the British Consul" but only managed a feeble "Engländer" where upon he became all smiles, thumped me on the back and I didn't have to pay. On-the-spot fines were the rule for all minor offences, even leaving litter and I carried one cigar butt all round Berlin and back to my hotel because I dared not drop it and could find no litter bin. Everything was efficient and orderly on the surface and although with hindsight it may seem unlikely that we could return mentally unscathed from two weeks in Nazi Germany at such a time, this is how it was; nothing yet had been really brought home to us.

· 11 ·

IN JANUARY 1937 we were concerned with another short opera season with various conductors as well as Beecham. Constant Lambert did "Manon Lescaut" – he was primarily a ballet conductor and always had difficulty in following singers; Stanford Robinson took "Die Fledermaus" but I did not play for him at that time; he was another conductor who listened to all the records and wondered why he could not get the same results as Toscanini. Both he and his brother Eric were extremely successful though I could never quite understand why. "Hansel and Gretel" was conducted by Lawrence Collingwood, a very competent and knowledgeable man who had worked in Russia before the Revolution, he was at Sadlers Wells and also the resident conductor of the Gramophone Company. Records of singers would often have on the label merely: "So-and-so with Orchestra" so a great deal of his work would get no recognition. Finally, there was a funny little man called Salfi who was rumoured to be an agent who had offered to get singers for Beecham on the cheap and so in return was allowed to conduct Verdi's "Un Ballo in Maschera" and Puccini's "Gianni Schicchi". He used to smile a great deal and hand round photographs of himself. In the pit he would stand there, grinning broadly as usual, giving no indication of when he was about to start conducting. Then suddenly away he would go, still smiling; it was obviously great fun for him, but not for us.

"Gianni Schicchi" and Strauss's "Salome" were given on the same evening, it made a very long programme but at least it wasn't "Elektra" and "Salome" together, as Beecham had originally planned; that would have been unendurable. The title role in "Salome" was taken by two different artists and one of them was so very glamorous that when she came on stage the orchestra all lost their places. Hans Knappertsbusch conducted the "Salome"; he was known to be lazy

52

and averse to rehearsing; we only went over a few passages in one rehearsal in the Crush Bar, followed by just one with the stage. He did not need more – he knew it, we knew it and our rapport was complete. He was tremendously tall and sat down all the time, giving a minimal beat, one in a bar or two if you were lucky. When he wanted to achieve a great crescendo at the very end of the opera he suddenly stood up and the effect on the orchestra was quite electrifying; we nearly blew the roof off the theatre. For years afterwards when "Salome" was being discussed people would ask: "Where you there the night that Knappertsbusch stood up?" It was the only time I played for him and a great experience so I was bitterly disappointed when I listened to a broadcast of his "Ring" from Bayreuth after the war and found it very ponderous and unyielding, the Siegfried in particular simply could not manage at the inflexible slow tempo.

In the April season Flagstad was back to delight us and it was our first "Ring" with Wilhelm Furtwängler. An extraordinary notice appeared on the board before the first performance of "Das Rheingold" to the effect that members of the orchestra were forbidden to cross their legs! Nothing was said and no concerted plot was laid but when Dr. Furtwängler came into the pit that evening every player whose instrument did not prevent him from doing so was sitting with his legs crossed. As soon as the maestro raised his baton they were all uncrossed. He apologized later, having realized that English orchestras could not be treated in that way.

The great man had a very strange beat, the only word to describe it is – wobbly. The Berlin Philharmonic, his own orchestra, had been trained to understand it but it was most unnerving for us to try to find the beat among the wobbles. For example: the opening of "Siegfried" has two bars timpani roll and then two bassoons come in, in thirds. Furtwängler would start quite steadily for two bars and then, just before the bassoon entry, he would begin to wobble and they didn't know where they were; poor Jack and George Alexandra would be sweating with terror. When the Berlin Philharmonic came over here and we were entertaining them after their concert I asked one of their players how they had managed to stay together when faced with this problem in the opening of Beethoven's "Coriolanus" overture. "We wait until we hear the first, faint scrape of the double bass and then we all play like hell" was his explanation. It was all to do with Furtwängler's dislike of the over-clear and over-precise, just as

53

pianists of Paderewski's generation would spread their chords into a ripple instead of playing them cleanly.

Furtwängler considered the "Ring" purely orchestrally, it seemed to me. He took no notice of the stage; the curtain got stuck and would not go up for the third act of "Die Walküre" so the Valkyries were singing away behind it but when the stage manager came to apologize afterwards the maestro had not even noticed. This encouraged the great tenor, Lauritz Melchior, who was the Siegmund, to have a little fun by holding his high notes for far too long because he knew that Furtwängler would just go on conducting, regardless.

On the whole, the pace of his "Ring" was a little quicker than we were used to, and thereby hangs a tale. Tuba or percussion players with a very large number of bars' rest would time them carefully, often with a stopwatch, so that they could relax – except of course for Jimmy Bradshaw, the timpanist, who was still counting with clacking dentures. Charlie Turner, the triangle player, had a very long wait for his first entry in "Rheingold" when the gold is seen for the first time so he would retire to the "Nag's Head" and stroll quietly back to take his place shortly before he was needed. On the first night of "Rheingold" with Furtwängler we became seriously alarmed as time was getting on and there was no sign of Charlie Turner. Now there were only a couple of bars to go – then came the sound of running feet in the passage under the stage, one bar – and the door to the pit opened, a hand came round, struck the triangle and vanished again. Next day all the stopwatches were out for a retiming.

Looking through the list of conductors for 1937 I see that the chorus-master, Robert Ainsworth – conductor with the Carl Rosa and husband of the contralto Muriel Brunskill – was "on" for at least one performance of "Carmen", probably because Beecham wanted a night off and almost certainly without a rehearsal. Bob and I were friendly, he would take me to lunch at the Savage Club and we would listen to records together. His preparation of the chorus was skilful and far-sighted: before a Beecham performance he would put them through their paces, trying to catch them out with every variation of tempo Sir Thomas might feel inclined to spring on them. When I said that Beecham had perfect tempo this applied to his ability to reproduce at will any tempo he had fixed – *if* he chose to do so. He could be quite unpredictable in this respect if the mood was upon him, but after Bob Ainsworth had prepared the chorus they were ready for anything.

That same season saw just two performances of a new work by Eugene Goossens, "Don Juan de Mañara", in a most beautiful production ablaze with blue and gold. There was a little serenade which earned a round of applause but otherwise the music was faceless, it was never revived and the event is only worth recording because it was the only new British opera to be put on in the pre-war Grand Season at the Garden in my time.

Beecham always liked to have about him an assistant, a tame expert or, to put it bluntly, a whipping-boy. For some extraordinary reason his choice in 1937 had fallen on Lionel Tertis, the violist. The first one I had known was Maurice Johnston, a cynical Lancastrian well able to take the strain, who became the Director of Music for BBC Northern in Manchester. Then for a while there was Eric Fenby, Delius' famous amanuensis, who seemed to me to look very uncomfortable and out of place. I can remember seeing him at Ealing Studios where we were making a film about Mozart with the huge actor John Loder, of all people, as the composer. Beecham was behaving in a very adolescent manner with a buxom and not unattractive singer called Enid James whom he had promoted from the chorus to small parts and with whom he was quite besotted. The orchestra were making ribald comments and poor Fenby with his rather puritanical outlook was desperately ill at ease. And now it was Lionel Tertis who knew nothing about opera. The first task Beecham set him was to bow and finger all the string parts. Now bowing was always done by the leader of the section and fingering is a highly individual matter. Tertis' idiosyncratic fingering – I understand he only rarely used his little finger – suited him as a soloist but, according to my friends in the strings, it did not suit anyone else and confusion ensued. He was also reputed to have suggested "bugging" the pit with a few microphones in order to catch any rebellious remarks from the strong left-wing element in the orchestra. Of course nothing was done about it but it all served to increase the growing feeling of "them and us" where the management were concerned. I think they were beginning to see Reds under the rostrum as, when I innocently arrived to rehearse in a chaste red tie given to me by a lady friend, Fred Laurence told me firmly I must not wear it again.

Tertis knew nothing about brass playing and made a wonderful howler at a recording session by wanting to know why the trombones could not all move their slides the same distance at the same time as it would look so much nicer. The odd one out was, of course, the bass trombone which is pitched in a different key so its slide position cannot be the same as that of the tenor trombones. After this it is understandable that the members of the stage band for "Aïda" on Coronation Day – with all three verses of the National Anthem, Elgar version, sung by Eva Turner and full chorus to start the proceedings – were far from pleased to be called an hour early in order to be "tuned" by Lionel Tertis. I know I arrived in a bad temper as I could not walk over Waterloo Bridge to the theatre because most of central London was closed for the Coronation ceremony; I had to take a Tube to Tottenham Court Road and walk back. We started to rehearse but it was not long before a trombone player who shall be nameless made an audible derogatory remark. Lionel Tertis had a very high voice, he jumped up and down and squeaked: "I will not be spoken to like that, I shall tell Sir Thomas." That did not worry anyone but to our amazement he added in even shriller tones: "I am the greatest viola player in the world!" It was left to the anonymous trombone to express what we all felt with a very vulgar noise.

When I became Librarian of the LPO in 1939 and began to have more contact with Sir Thomas I sometimes felt that he had it in mind to add me to his personal band of scurrying slaves and I was determined to resist it to the last. At the beginning of the war all his music had been removed from the Opera House and stored in an unused showroom in Denman Street, belonging to Boosey and Hawkes. We were rehearsing a Mozart Violin Concerto with Thomas Matthews who had brought his set of parts, but Beecham always preferred to use his own with all his markings. He summoned me to the platform.

"Mr. Savage, I must have my own parts for this concerto."

"I'm very sorry, Sir Thomas but it's not possible."

"Not possible?" he echoed in total disbelief.

"It's Sunday today," I explained. The store, of course, was closed.

"I don't care if it's Doomsday, I must have the parts at once."

"Even if it were Doomsday, you still couldn't have them" I replied doggedly and walked off the platform.

Berta Geissmar's face was a study in horror and amazement but "Tommy" did not make any more fuss and later she confided to me in her usual affectionate way: "Richard, you bloody fool that *is* the way to do it, after all!"

"The trouble is," said Harold Holt, the impresario, on the same occasion, "no one had ever said 'no' to Beecham." The combination of Sir Thomas's wealth and title with his brilliance and wicked tongue inclined people to be sycophantic and to yield to his every whim, which was bound to have a detrimental effect on his character. This may well have been why he had difficulty in achieving results with orchestras other than his own where the players were hand-picked because they understood him and "did it his way".

Before he went to the States shortly after this Beecham asked me in a somewhat vague way to look after the copyrights of his various arrangements and he would pay me a hundred pounds. I knew he never would and did nothing about it; subsequently his total ingratitude to Dr. Geissmar who *had* looked after his interests most faithfully during his absence made me very glad that I had learned to survive.

· 12 ·

1938, THE year of Munich, was the first time I played for Erich Kleiber. This short, thick-set, bald man with the piercing eyes had such a powerful personality that he could inspire devotion in the most hardened and cynical players and in return he was immensely considerate of us and our welfare. I was not playing in his first opera, "Flying Dutchman" but happened to be deputizing for someone at a Saturday evening rehearsal after the others had just finished not one but two three-hour rehearsals of "Fidelio" with Beecham. It did not take Kleiber long to discover why everyone was so totally exhausted and incapable; he sent us all home and called the rehearsal for Sunday morning which meant double money and caused the management to wring their hands. At any time, if he felt no more could be achieved, he was quite content to end a rehearsal early but while we were working it was always a period of intense concentration which was at the same time tremendously stimulating and enjoyable.

Rehearsals were so few in those days that it would not be until he returned in the 1950s that he would explain "Rosenkavalier" to us in great detail, but to play it for him was an immediate revelation. The wonderful score can too often turn into a thick swirl of sound but with Kleiber it became totally translucent with every theme and motif delicately visible and the lift and lilt he gave to the Viennese waltz has never been surpassed. He not only ennabled more of the words to be heard than ever before but also pointed out to us esoteric musical comments in the score that we were unaware of: at the Marschallin's levée the sellers of puppies are protesting that the little pets are house-trained (zimmerrein) but a descending scales on the violins and oboes indicates plainly that they have in fact just piddled on the carpet. He would also maintain that it is made clear in the score that Leopold, Baron Ochs' body-servant, is indeed his bastard son, but I have not been able to work that one out and it could well have been one of his dead-pan jokes. He was always imperturbable; I was playing on the famous night when Lotte Lehmann as the Marschallin burst into tears during her monologue in Act I, left the stage and ran straight into the arms of Norman Feasey, then a young repetiteur, crying: "I can't sing, I've lost my voice!" Rumours were rife – a relative had been taken to a concentration camp, a young lover had left her – the real reason was never known but the Marschallin's monologue would certainly have been agonizingly apposite for an ageing woman who had just been jilted. Miraculously, Hilde Konetzni was in the audience and was able to replace her after a short interval; Kleiber never turned a hair but it did not make for the most sparkling performance that night! This first experience of working for him was all too brief and it was to be eleven years before I would see him again and more than thirty before Carlos, the little boy I saw peering over into the pit and who, his father told us, was ruining him by insisting on playing the pin-tables in the Strand, was to return as a brilliant conductor in his own right.

We did get one more performance than we expected as Richard Tauber, who was singing Belmonte in "Il Seraglio", fell ill after the first night so "Rosenkavalier" was substituted which meant great agitation for Berta Geissmar who had to get all the singers back. It was also the day of the party to celebrate the recent wedding of John Cruft, the cor anglais,* and I arrived in the middle of the afternoon in full evening dress.

"Why on earth are you dressed like that, Richard?" enquired the bridegroom. He obviously thought I did not know what to wear on such occasions.

"You're going to have to get into yours in a minute," I retorted. "You are on tonight – it's Rosenkavalier." And, of course, he had to be there, but after the excitement of the party he kept falling asleep and I had to wake him up at vital moments. (He strenuously denies this, insisting that he had merely closed his eyes to rest them.)

There was considerable uncertainty as to whether we would have a 1939 season at all and, although it did materialize, it was in many ways a strange one and the feeling of unreality was enhanced by Beecham's latest passion for sound equipment and amplification, personified by Mr. Perkins, "the man from Marconi" as he liked to call

*Later Head of the Music Section of the Arts Council.

him. The harpsichord for the recitatives in "Don Giovanni" was to be placed in the scene dock instead of in the pit, together with four string players who were to sustain the chords in harmonies realized by Basil Cameron and the whole exercise, conducted by Signor Cimara, one of the repetiteurs, was to be relayed over loud-speakers to the auditorium. Of course, any scene-shifting noises or comments from rude stage hands came out loud and clear as well, while in the scene dock poor Cimara could see nothing and hear very little; before closed-circuit television this sort of thing was virtually impossible.

The wind and trombones who accompany the Don's dinner invitation to the statue of the Commendatore usually play backstage but in this last mad season we were placed behind a gauze in an alcove in the pit; on the opening night Beecham forgot on which side we were hidden, turned the wrong way to give us our lead – and we never came in. The supper music is normally played on stage, (13/6d extra then) and one had to memorize it, which I found difficult, so I was relieved at first when Charlie Moor decided to put us at the side of the stage but behind the scenery it was pitch dark so we couldn't read the parts and once again the long-suffering Cimara had no contact with the maestro in the pit.

A repetiteur's lot was not a happy one; it was not unusual to find one of them up a high ladder with his eye on a hole in the scenery, waving his arms in unison with the conductor as and when he could see him, this in turn being relayed by a second repetiteur at the foot of the ladder to the players at the side of the stage. None of this led to good ensemble playing but it was all part of the daily round for the music staff.

There were always at least two Italian coaches, two German and a prompter for each language. A few Englishmen came and went; they were at a distinct disadvantage as with our very short annual season they found it hard to gain sufficient experience, one notable exception being that distinguished coach, Norman Feasey, who arrived in the winter of 1936 sporting a memorable green pork pie hat, and whose services are still available to the Opera house in 1984.

I did not have much contact with the Italians and, apart from the hardworking Cimara who, I am glad to say, had a chance to conduct "La Traviata" in 1939 – and very competently he did it – I only recall a certain Signor Foranini whose Italian blood apparently got the better of him while conducting Marie Goossens as the off-stage harp in

"Traviata", causing him to make unwelcome advances to her; he was supposed to have been put on the first train back to Italy by her husband, Fred Laurence the next morning – he certainly vanished quite suddenly!

The German repetiteurs wore white coats in the theatre, like doctors; I became friendly with both of them in the final pre-war season. There was Karlheinrich Koch, a delightful red-haired man who became head of Cologne Radio after the war, and Horst Walter from Dresden who also survived the war but became a Benedictine monk at Regensburg in Austria. We used to repair to Schmidt's in Charlotte Street after performances and talk shop for hours. I took Horst Walter to Hampstead Heath to see a splendid display of pyrotechnics with massed bands playing Handel's "Music for the Royal Fireworks". It was a wonderful summer night and he was greatly impressed; but another occasion impressed him in a very different and disagreeable manner. It was the night Basil Cameron was unaccountably allowed to conduct "Tristan". He was not an opera conductor and after the Prelude, which he knew from the concert hall, we were all literally wallowing like a ship head-on to the wind. Matters were not helped by his conducting style, once described by the composer John Gardner* as "A man trying to get out of a sack." At one point we really seemed about to sink without a trace when Horace (Jimmy) Green, the cor anglais, who had dozed off from a blend of beer and bewilderment, woke up suddenly and started to play so for a moment we all recognized a place where we might be. Finally we did reach the Liebestod, concert-hall stuff once more; Basil Cameron took off his glasses, cheered up and we all finished the opera more or less together. Horst Walter was in the prompt box that night and he staggered out to meet us afterwards, holding his head. "In Dresden," he complained "we have an emergency button in the prompt box and at such a terrible moment one would press it to bring down the curtain – but tonight, I looked – and there was no button!" It took us most of the evening to console him.

Not only Cimara and Basil Cameron but also Wynn Reeves, who had led the Opera orchestra in the 1920s and had now joined the LPO, "had a go" at one performance of "Aïda" and, fortunately, made a very good job of it. But why was Beecham delegating so much? Had he

*Composer of the opera "The Moon and Sixpence"

lost interest as he sensed the approach of the end of life as he had always known it? Was he metaphorically throwing his baton away to whoever could catch it, like a bride's bouquet? The whole atmosphere certainly seemed strange to me and Sir Thomas more than usually capricious. There were happy moments, as when he suggested that we while away the time while Charlie Moor sorted out something on stage in "Götterdämmerung" by playing the "Blue Danube" – and painful ones like the rehearsal of "The Bartered Bride". The cast consisted of Richard Tauber and an experienced company of Austrian singers but nothing they did was right and the leading soprano ultimately burst into tears. Tauber came forward and said gently, with his charming smile: "I am afraid, Sir Thomas, we have been singing it incorrectly for so long that it will take us a little while to get used to the right way." After that things began to get better but I am glad to look back on at least one entirely rewarding experience that season, playing for Felix Weingartner.

Weingartner conducted "Tannhäuser" and "Parsifal". Slim and quiet, impeccably dressed, with a rare, rewarding smile, he was the embodiment of Richard Strauss's dictum that it is the orchestra who should sweat, not the conductor. His beat was minimal but we sweated for him, filled with inevitable awe as we looked at a man who had been present at the first rehearsals of "Parsifal" at Bayreuth and could tell us with authority: "This is what the Master wanted here." At certain points in the work where there were particular chords in the wind and strings he would direct that they should overlap, rather like the sustaining pedal on the piano, so that instead of being clear-cut they would melt into each other. This authentic style of playing such passages has not been observed by later conductors, but we had the uncanny feeling of being in direct link with those first performances.

When the season ended I went on a camping holiday with Hilda and my parents to Tyneham, a Dorset village later to be totally destroyed in the rehearsals for D Day. For days we were shrouded in thick mist which finally lifted to reveal the entire fleet off Weymouth, waiting to be reviewed by the King. I walked up to the tiny village post office to collect the mail and the postmistress gave me a black look as she handed me a postcard from Germany – my last news of Horst Walter for many years. Everyone was hurrying back to London and we had to stand all the way in the train while one thought was uppermost in my mind: what would happen about next season?

Part Two

TOURING WITH THE LONDON PHILHARMONIC ORCHESTRA
1939–46

· 13 ·

"HELLO— Fred? It's Richard. What's the situation?"

   "Nothing, as far as I know."

   "Nothing? Aren't we going to . . .?"

   "No. Everything's cancelled."

   "But . . ."

   "That's all I know. Don't bother me now, Dick."

The receiver clicked back and, now I come to think of it, that was the last I ever heard of Fred Laurence. Till then I had indulged in hopeful fantasies of programmes where "Land of Hope and Glory" would be played repeatedly, thus ensuring constant employment for myself; but now I had to face it, I was jobless and practically penniless, never having understood how people managed to save. Hilda had a fair amount of teaching, mostly at Watford, so the flat in Highgate would go and we would move in with my parents, then to rooms in Watford and ultimately to a small house there but, although I did not then know it, for the next five years my home was to be any room where I could rent a bed and my possessions my instruments and a suitcase.

Optimistically, I decided to join the Auxiliary Fire Service but, after tramping the whole of North London for some time, I realized the sad truth that they were already over-subscribed and had no need of me. I had always been interested in wireless, constantly making my own sets as a boy, and I found a course at Kew where one could train to be a radio operator with the Forces. The Navy appealed to me and I must have mentioned this possibility at home for my mother informed all the family that I was to be a sailor and my Aunt Daisy promptly knitted me a vast sea-going sweater. After I had started the course I discovered that everyone was graduating into the Air Force.

Meanwhile, unknown to me, the new future of the Orchestra was already being shaped. At a meeting on September 18th 1939 the old

65

company had been liquidated, many members under contract still being owed back pay. Leon Goossens, for example, told me that he was still owed £80 – a considerable sum then – so as an extra without a contract I had benefitted for once. A small number of key players left at once to take up contracts already secretly negotiated with the BBC Salon Orchestra at Evesham but, unexpectedly, a handful of orchestral members emerged as a potential committee willing to try to run the orchestra themselves. They were: Charles Gregory (first horn), tall and with a good presence which made him an ideal candidate for the office of Chairman – although personally I never felt at ease with him; Thomas Russell (viola), pale, moustached, tubercular, with bright dark eyes – he was to emerge as the man of the hour in the office of Secretary; tiny fiery Francis ("Buller") Bradley (third horn); Reg Morley (first violin) and Frank Stead (first trombone), a Yorkshireman of whom Tom Russell wrote* "He looked upon speech as a necessity rather than a pleasure." To start with, Jack Alexandra, the first bassoon who had been kind to me when I first joined the orchestra, was also a member. He was very much in love at the time with a handsome brunette called Mignon Pareira who had been the Opera House secretary and he now wanted her to become the Orchestral Secretary. When he could not arrange this for her he left the committee although he remained with the orchestra until a couple of years later when he simply and suddenly disappeared. He just failed to turn up for a concert and his brother George had to take over first bassoon while I played the second bassoon part on the bass clarinet. Later, Jack reappeared as first bassoon with the Philharmonia Orchestra.

The first inkling I had of the rebirth of the LPO was a phone call from Charlie Gregory saying that they were "trying to get things going again" and that they had thought of me as the best person to come and sort out the music needed for the first series of concerts. So I met the Directors at the Opera House and was duly appointed Librarian. I was to be paid as a principal which would mean a delightful £2 8s for every concert as I would always be in attendance, though if I happened to play the bass clarinet I would have to throw that in for nothing. Actually, I think I used to get paid twice for recording sessions, as player and librarian. Things were certainly looking up financially and it was from that date that I began to add considerably to my collection

*Thomas Russell: Philharmonic Decade.

66

of scores, acquiring them from music shops all over England as we toured, though it is sad that those on war-time paper have worn so badly and are now yellowed and crumbling.

Beecham's library was all stored on the sixth floor at the Opera House and at one point old Mr. Ballard, the machinist, decided for reasons best known to himself to switch off the lift and I had to carry everything down six flights of stairs. At first we were still able to rehearse in the theatre but it was not available for long and soon Beecham's scores were all removed to the Boosey and Hawkes storeroom in Denman Street which I mentioned earlier. The orchestra office was very briefly at Empire House, Piccadilly and then at Boosey and Hawkes in Regent Street. Here, on January 1st 1940, my friend Felix Aprahmian, now music critic of the "Sunday Times" but then a youthful conscientious objector with what Tom Russell called "the wildest enthusiasm" for music, joined the staff as assistant to the Secretary and spent his first day making out the £1 share certificates for the new venture which was to be known as Musical Culture Ltd. He was also to assist the directors in programme making which meant devoting all his energies to trying to get his favourite works performed. He was to accompany us on many a tour, invariably wearing his tin hat which looked wonderfully incongruous with his suave Armenian beard. An inveterate Francophile, his enthusiasm was also directed towards the promotion of concerts of French music during and after the war. With the LPO he tells me that he agreed to accept a salary of £3 10s a week as that was all the air raid wardens received.

The cash-flow problems of those early days must have been appalling – how were train fares, hotels, printing and so on as well as salaries to be paid for entirely out of the proceeds of the concerts? I am thankful that I had no part in this awesome task. As Beecham's ideas for raising more money were purely hypothetical and poor Berta Geissmar was reputedly thinking of selling her violin to help (I have no doubt she would have done it, too,) the first concerts were largely backed by the wealthy Sydney Beer who inevitably had to conduct a proportion of them. The first concert on October 1st under Beecham was reported by Tom Russell to be a great success but he added rather unkindly that the subsequent ones under Beer were very much less satisfactory, especially as the latter insisted on programmes requiring a large orchestra and many extra players. I only remember a brisk opening tour of Cardiff, Swansea, Cheltenham and Southampton; it was still the phoney war and everything seemed much as usual. Before long, however, there were signs of change. Russell was a dedicated Communist and not only did the orchestra represent, as it were, the Party to which we owed unquestioning loyalty – it was J. B. Priestley who was to call us the London Philharmonic Soviet in a fund-raising speech – but music was now to be brought to the masses. In between Queen's Hall concerts we would visit unheard-of spots like Croydon, Wembley, Watford, Walthamstow and Chatham, whereas before the war many orchestral noses, probably including mine, had been turned up on the isolated occasion when we played at Finsbury Park Empire and there had been mutterings of: "*Not* the sort of audience we are accustomed to play for."

Once, when I was sharing a taxi with Russell and Charlie Gregory, Tom expounded his doctrine, explaining that for him this was the only way of life.

"Of course, it's different for you, Dick" he said kindly. "You went to a public school." It was indeed different for me but, politics apart, at that moment and in those circumstances Tom Russell was the man we needed and he was able for a considerable time to inspire us with a tremendous feeling of solidarity and a willingness to work without holidays under conditions of considerable hardship because it was our own form of National Service; and that, in fact, is how Ernest Bevin viewed it when he became Minister of Manpower.

My clearest memory of the 1939 autumn concerts is of two performances of Weinberger's "Variations and Fugue on Under the Spreading Chestnut Tree." The composer had been inspired by a newsreel of George VI singing and miming with a boys' summer camp; the work had great success in the States and Ralph Hawkes persuaded Beecham to do it. An organ pedal was required for one solitary note and I suggested to the Directors that I should have a shot at it. I had never played the organ in my life but the Queen's Hall organ had a crescendo pedal which did all the work for me. There was to be a second performance at Central Hall, Westminster but here the organ was entirely different and at rehearsal the wretched thing appeared to be taking over from me. As the noise got louder and louder Sir Thomas could be heard shouting: "Good Heavens! Mr. Savage has gone native, will someone stop him!" and Bill Coleman, the third trombone who had saved the day all those years ago when Felix White fell off the organ loft at Covent Garden, rushed up horror-struck to explain to me what I should do. I managed all right at the concert, became over-confident and tried it again when we recorded the piece later with Constant Lambert. My unrestrained decibels brought the recording engineer out of his booth like a jack-in-the-box, spitting with fury and crying: "Don't you know you should never use an open diapason in a recording session?" I didn't of course, but I do now and I have never tried to play the organ since that day.

Beecham would soon be leaving us for America, committing the orchestra to the care of the audience in an emotional speech after his farewell all-Sibelius concert in honour of the Finns who had just been invaded, but we made quite a few records with him for EMI that first winter of the war and they were gradually released over the next two years; on the basis of this, as Russell pointed out in his book, no doubt future historians will be arguing that he was still with us in 1942. Weingartner too came over from Switzerland for the last time and we recorded Mozart Symphony no. 39 and Brahms' Second Symphony with him. There was some confusion over the labels for the Brahms and this was credited for some time to the London Symphony Orchestra.

Now I was always in attendance as librarian I had the opportunity of hearing some of his reminiscences during the break in recording. He told me how he had been present at the first performance of the Brahms Second Symphony in Berlin, being invited afterwards to a party at the Adlon Hotel where, as a rather earnest student, he had been very shocked when Brahms and Joachim, the violinist, became exceedingly drunk, danced on the table and finally had to be locked up for the night. Once again the great names of the past became living, fallible humans for me and all the more interesting because of it, and once again I marvelled at Weingartner whose apparently inexpressive beat produced such expressive playing, the fundamental beat and rhythm being so inherent in his whole body and not merely in the stick that the orchestra felt at the same time absolute freedom to play and the constant controlling flow of music. He would keep a slow tempo going throughout a long movement such as the second movement of Beethoven's Second Symphony, without ever letting it become bogged down, maintaining always a vital inner pulse. It is without hesitation that I count him as the first of my personal five giants.

· 14 ·

BEECHAM'S contact with the Directors, as the committee liked to be called, was short-lived and his attitude towards them one of mild surprise. They for their part were anxious to prove their capabilities and in this connection I was interested to find myself mentioned as a protagonist in an event at an early war-time concert in Liverpool which I had quite forgotten. In his "Philharmonic Decade" Russell recounts how the part for one piece was missing from one desk of double-bass players – and I can well imagine them sitting there, arms folded, having made no attempt to check their music or to go to look for it. Sir Thomas was naturally becoming disturbed by the sight of these two idle fellows staring at him so Russell finally decided to put down his viola and bow as quietly as possible and tiptoe off, in full view of the audience, in search of help. Apparently he was much relieved to bump into me immediately when I "might have been hundreds of yards away" and I laid my hand at once upon the missing part. I expect I just gave him a spare but Sir Thomas's opinion of the efficiency of the committee was supposed to have improved from that moment. I should like to think so but, knowing Sir Thomas, I must be given leave to doubt it! I know only too well what must have happened. The parts all have to be made up for each desk in their cardboard folders and it is rather like the moment in the "Wind in the Willows" where the Water Rat is assembling the heaps of weapons for the attack on Toad Hall and running round muttering: "A belt for the rat, a belt for the Mole, a belt for the Badger, a cutlass for the Rat, a cutlass for the Mole . . ." A moment's distraction and two of the same part get into one folder; I expect it was somewhere on the platform all the time. I am only surprised that this sort of thing did not happen far more often.

The music was actually set out by the orchestra porter, Wally

Knight, who had been with the LPO since its inception. A gloomy little Cockney sparrow of a man with hands always blue with cold, he was never seen to wear gloves and must have been incredibly tough for his job was certainly no sinecure. Single-handed he had to hump everything heavy: music, music-stands, rostra, drums, double basses, harp, celeste from wherever we were to wherever we had to go next, whether it was from below stage at the Opera House to the first floor Crush Bar or from a concert hall to a station, on and off trains and from station to concert hall again. He was given to sardonic grumbling and curious retorts which I have never heard from anyone else, for example, if one happened to ejaculate "Oh, balls!" to any of his observations he would reply lugubriously: "Only cook one, I won't be home for tea." One of his perennial grumbles was that if he was obliged to lay on a little extra help he would have to pay for it out of his own pocket, although I imagine he eventually managed to get some of it back, with difficulty. When the Festival Hall was built after the war he put in for a job there and a less strenuous life. It was there that I last saw him in 1956 when he announced with his usual gloomy relish: "I see your friend Kleiber's died, then," unaware that the news came as a total shock to me – not that I think it would have made any difference if he had realized!

In 1940, with Beecham gone to the States and Sir Adrian Boult very much involved with his own BBC Orchestra, conductors were rather thin on the ground and we fell mainly into the hands of Malcolm Sargent, Basil Cameron and Charles Hambourg, a stout cheerful extrovert married to a very thin wealthy wife and so probably able to put money into the business. He was a rather rough and ready conductor, known to the orchestra as the Stepney Slasher and inclined to select very long programmes full of loud and jolly pieces. I remember him falling off the platform once at a concert in Blackburn; we played stolidly on until he rejoined us, fortunately not much hurt.

It seems strange that my memories of the terrible spring and summer of 1940 should be so fitful but as the chief, or sole merit of these reminiscences is to be their veracity I have no intention of adding any fictitious trimmings to heighten the interest. In the April of 1940 we gave a series of three Beethoven concerts with the three conductors I have just referred to and as they were successful they were followed in May by three all-Bach concerts which were not so well received, probably because of the general gloom and anxiety at that time over

71

the invasion of Norway. The Anglo-French Festival which was to follow was even more ill-fated as the French Government had capitulated only twenty-four hours before the first concert which turned out to be the only one we gave. I remember playing in Ibert's ballet suite "Diane de Poitiers" and Basil Cameron conducting the Marseillaise in an atmosphere of great emotion. Then my next flash of memory is of a June Saturday in Reading, walking through the town to the concert while train after train disgorged the hapless survivors of Dunkirk into the streets, presumably to some assembly point but they seemed totally bewildered and kept trying to explain to us in cafés and on street corners: "We had no air cover – we were just sitting ducks – there was no air cover at all." What could we say to them? Everyone felt as they did, lost, humiliated and uncertain of the future.

One thing was certain, money for the orchestra had to be raised at all costs and on July 18th 1940 the "Musical Manifesto" concert was given at Queen's Hall with Boult conducting Elgar's "Cockaigne" Overture, Basil Cameron conducting Eileen Joyce playing the Grieg Piano Concerto and the Second Symphony of Sibelius with Sargent. J. B. Priestley was by now the champion of the orchestra, his speech received wide coverage in the Press and thousands of people who had not been at the concert began also to support us. One of the most successful publicity ideas was the monthly magazine "Philharmonic Post", on sale at all our concerts and which featured regular articles on various "orchestral personalities". By 1941 it was personality number nineteen and my turn. I was portrayed twice, once sitting very stiffly in front of the bass clarinet as though I had no idea what to do with it and in the second photograph busy copying orchestral parts and smoking furiously. The readers were informed: "His approach to the duties of Librarian is more artistic than routine; it would be no serious criticism to say that he brings more enthusiasm and imagination to the task than business-like methods." I have no doubt that my staff at the Opera House until my retirement in 1982 would say cheerfully that I had never changed – I left the business-like methods to them and all was well. The orchestral fans were also told that I most enjoyed occupying my leisure with the copying of music: "a task he performs with all the care and pleasure of an artist" and forty-four years later that also is as true as ever. I cannot remember when I first started copying though my first professional work came at the beginning of the war for firms like Boosey and Hawkes, Chester's and the Oxford Press, but I always

72

Richard Temple Savage
aged 21

1935 Frederick Laurence,
Sir Thomas Beecham's
orchestral manager
(*Courtesy of Marie
Goossens*)

1935 Oda Slobodskaya in
"Koanga" (Delius)
(*Courtesy of A. Console, his
only surviving relative – a
sister*)

1935 Felix Weingartner
(1863–1942) first of the
"five giants" (*Courtesy of
"Opera" magazine*)

1942 Sir Henry Wood

1947 Wedding Day. 92° in
the shade!

Dame Eva Turner in
"Turandot" (*Photo by
Baron, courtesy of "Opera"
magazine*)

1947 Karl Rankl Musical
Director R.O.H.
1946–1951 (*Courtesy of
"Opera" magazine*)

1949 Silveri, Schwarzkopf, Schock and Geraint Evans Act II "La Bohème"
(*Photo by Roger Wood, courtesy of "Opera" magazine*)

1945 Beecham with L.P.O. in Brussels with Jean Pougnet laughing on left
"his fans were many and devoted"

1951 Erich Kleiber, second of the "five giants" (1890–1956)

1953–54 Stage Band "Der Freischütz" with Richard Temple Savage on right

Sir William Walton. "As I remember him" (*Photo by Douglas Glass*)

Tim Killar "one of the great eccentrics of the Opera House" (*Photo by Reg Wilson*)

Richard Temple Savage in Music Library, 45 Floral Street (*Photo by Reg Wilson*)

1955 Peter Pears and Elsie Morison in "The Bartered Bride" (*Photo by Houston Rogers, Theatre Museum, courtesy of "Opera" magazine*)

strove consciously to make my work resemble a printed page as closely as possible. I felt that Rafael Kubelik gave me the final accolade in the 1950s when he asked me to copy his father's works, saying that I was "one of the two best copyists in Europe". The other, I believe, was a Pole – I should have liked to meet him.

Copying a valuable score on tour during the year of air-raids was quite a responsibility. I was engaged for some time on the orchestral parts of Walton's Violin Concerto, keeping the score under my bed and sending regular reassuring postcards to Willy at Ashby St. Leger where he was living with the beautiful Lady Wimborne. We did not have an inordinate amount of free time on the endless tours as if we were not rehearsing or snatching a meal of dried egg, Spam or baked beans on toast we were generally in the train on our way to our next port of call, but we did spend several days at a time in the larger cities and then, after I had seen every available film at the local cinemas, I would retire to the Commercial Room of my hotel, set out with little cubicled desks rather like a post office, where the commercial travellers would make up their accounts and reports in the evenings – and there I would copy peacefully.

I was also occupied for some time in selecting, at the request of Ralph Hawkes, difficult passages for the clarinet for three volumes of orchestral studies from the current repertory as the old pre-war Breitkopf and Härtel ones were both out of date and out of print. I was never really satisfied with the new volumes as Ralph Hawkes' idea was to sell them chiefly to High School orchestras in the United States where, he insisted, the A clarinet was unknown and so everything should be transposed for B flat clarinet. My contention was that it would be better to sell A clarinets to the High School pupils as if and when they ever met the complete part on the music stand it would be as written by the composer and not transposed for them! As a compromise they were finally published with the transpositions for B flat clarinet in small type below the A clarinet extracts, something with which I refused to have anything to do and which earned considerable criticsm from players and teachers. Nevertheless, they proved very popular and are still bringing me a few royalties after forty years. I should have liked to bring the selection up to date with a volume of the post-war composers such as Britten and Shostakovitch and was constantly being asked when I was going to do this. I finally approached Boosey and Hawkes myself with the suggestion, only to find that another publisher had been quicker off the mark, it was a great disappointment.

Shortly after the Musical Manifesto in 1940 an unlikely *deus ex machina* appeared to rescue us in the shape of one of the Big Band leaders, Jack Hylton. He ran the Empire Music Halls all over the country and was willing to put us on, a week in each town, in programmes of our own choosing without any extra turns such as magicians or dancers – apart from a singer who would render Vera Lynn style numbers in the interval and a selection of popular piano pieces to be played by Eileen Joyce. She was a creature of varying moods, constantly up and down and complaining that she did not feel able to give of her best that day. She carried a capacious handbag which coarser members of the orchestra insisted must be full of ladies' hygienic requirements as she was so frequently below par. It was very much a male chauvinist world.

A stage set was constructed for us and travelled with us and Malcolm Sargent would introduce the pieces simply to the audience. He had a great flair for this sort of thing and had always been connected with the Robert Mayer Children's Concerts. I can still hear him talking about Tschaikowsky's "Romeo and Juliet: "And if you listen carefully you can hear Juliet's little heart beating beneath her dress!" The audiences loved him. In spite of all these concessions to popular taste an occasional protest was heard, like the little old lady in the one and sixpennys in Edinburgh who called out during a performance of Dvořak's "New World" Symphony: "Can ye no play something *cheery*?"

Our first Jack Hylton concert in Glasgow on August 12th 1940 coincided with the first Blitz on London and we all hurried, panic-stricken, to phone our families but no one could get through as the London telephone exchange had been hit. We had to continue on our tour to Manchester and Birmingham before eventually returning to London to find out what had happened. At the end of that first Glasgow week we all had to go up to Charlie Gregory's room in the Grand Hotel (where six years later I would be staying, again on tour but also on honeymoon) to collect our money, all laid out on the bed in little envelopes. One or two timid knocks were heard as unsophisticated members returned, mumbling in an embarrassed way: "It seems to be short – there's only one note." They had never seen a ten-pound note before and were expecting two fivers; and they

82

were Scottish notes, on which we would lose eighteenpence if we cashed them South of the Border!

On our way to Manchester for the next week of Jack Hylton concerts we stopped off in Blackpool for a Sunday evening concert as well and ended the programme with Tschaikowsky's "1812" Overture, complete with explosive cannon effects unwisely laid on by Basil Cameron to liven things up. After the news of the London Blitz the audience were understandably a trifle jumpy and almost panicked, several of them trying to rush out as it began to get noisier and having to be restrained by friends with stronger nerves. We ourselves needed stronger nerves in Manchester where the Palace Theatre had just been vacated by a circus and the smell under the stage was enough to knock you over. I was thankful to move on to Birmingham where my favourite Aunt Dollie and Uncle Ernest lived in quiet respectability in Bournville. I visited them but did not like to ask if I could stay as Aunt Dollie was greatly worried by wartime shortages and would announce firmly: "You can't get it now" whenever the simplest item of food was mentioned, a habit she was never to lose, even after the war.

By the time we left Birmingham I had managed to contact my family and know that they had survived the Blitz, but we were soon off again on further Hylton tours and I remember being sorely tried by the touring manager Jack Hylton sent out with us. He was a very pleasant man but he insisted that the best dressing room next to the stage was always his by right, and this was where I would have liked to store the music. Sometimes I succeeded in getting a room fairly near but at others I might be staggering up and downstairs, heavily laden. There was nothing to be done, he looked very shocked when I suggested we might change, but before long we began to promote more of our own concerts and acquired as business manager none less than Harold Fielding whom I suppose everyone would now think of in connection with great musicals at Drury Lane. I had met him first when I was playing in the Stock Exchange Orchestra in the early thirties and he came on the platform as a very small boy in a Fauntleroy suit and played a very dashing piece on his violin – "Air Varié" by Rode. Then at the beginning of the war the LPO had given a concert in the Odeon Cinema in Woking where he lived and the conductor, Sir Adrian Boult, the Directors and I were asked back to tea. He was not to stay with us long, unfortunately – no doubt he and Tom Russell would have seen things very differently. When I came to live in Woking in

83

1949 I would meet him on the station sometimes and he told me how Russell had informed him that the age of the impresario was over! So Harold left to prove him wrong.

Harold Fielding's successor was Adolf Borsdorf, the viola player whom I also remembered as a pre-war film "fixer". Their different approaches to life can best be illustrated by the little exchange of views I heard one evening (in Weston-super-Mare to be precise) when Adolf asked Harold over a drink: "What do you think of that smashing bit of goods in the box office?" and Fielding replied, with equal enthusiasm: "She seems *very* efficient to me!"

· 15 ·

WHILE we were playing the Empires we could at least be sure of a full week in one place but as we began to promote more of our own concerts we dashed continually from one town to the next and sometimes back to the first one as we could not give a concert on a Sunday in Scotland, so if we were playing there on a Saturday night we would nip over the Border for a Sunday performance in England and then back again on the Monday. Life was an endless succession of anonymous, unappetizing hotel rooms, so I was thankful to be spending a rare night at home in Wimbledon on Saturday May 10th 1941, after playing in the "Dream of Gerontius" with Sargent at the Queen's Hall.

On Sunday morning I set off up to town again for a rehearsal with Morris Miles, a good conductor with a bad temper but who seemed all set for success at the time. As the train drew into Waterloo I noticed that the sunny air was filled with ashes and, walking up from Oxford Circus station, I could see the smoking ruins of Queen's Hall and the stooping figures of my colleagues, searching for their instruments in the charred rubble. Momentarily I caught a glimpse of Tom Russell standing with a stunned expression on his face, but then he turned briskly on his heel and set off back to the office to start reorganizing everything; he was always at his best in a crisis. The gutter outside the stage door was running with water from the fire hoses and, almost before I had time to become anxious about it, I saw my bass clarinet floating along. I opened the heavy leather case and there it was, damp but perfectly playable. At the same time Cedric Sharp was finding his cello case but it must have been exposed for longer to the intense heat as when he opened it the cello had completely disintegrated, all the glue having melted. I am glad to say that he was later able to have it completely reconstructed.

Fortunately, most fiddle players took their instruments home with them and the woodwind were in the habit of leaving theirs in a small band-room near the stage door – still furnished with rows of long wooden pegs where previous generations of players had hung up their top hats – and the firemen had been able to throw the contents of this room quickly into the street. The music and heavy instruments left in position on the platform and those in the main band-room underneath took the full heat of the fire bombs.

People hurried home for spare instruments and the Duke's Hall at the Royal Academy of Music was taken over for the concert; we took it in turns to stand outside the ruins and direct the audience to the new venue. The Academy must certainly have helped in the matter of the larger instruments that day but shortly afterwards an appeal was broadcast on the BBC and the offices of Boosey and Hawkes were piled high for some time with quantities of decrepit old violins and so on. It was a touching response but I don't think they were able to make real use of many of them.

In view of all the excitement perhaps it is not so surprising that I have no recollection of what we played but I know we lost the music for the Grieg Piano Concerto so I know that must have been on the programme and the Academy lent us as much as they could of the works originally to be played. The Grieg had been borrowed from a certain Teddy O'Brien, a very garrulous Irishman with wild grey hair, formerly librarian of the London Symphony Orchestra, who owned a large private collection of music. He was of great help to me when I was forming the LPO library, selling me some of his duplicates or indicating to me where a set of parts could be found; however, on this occasion he was not pleased with me and demanded compensation for the loss of his Grieg Piano Concerto, which of course he had not a hope of getting. One always needed to be able to spend some time with him as he had an inexhaustible fund of rather lengthy funny stories, at which he always roared with laughter himself so they took even longer to tell. One of his most prized possessions was the original Russian orchestration of Schumann's "Carnaval" by Rimsky-Korsakov and others. When he hired it out for the ballet at the Opera House before the war he would creep into the pit, set all the parts out himself and then sit there in a corner throughout the performance to keep an eye on them until he could collect them all up again at the end.

I suppose it is inevitable that, apart from landmarks like the burning of Queen's Hall or the bombing of Coventry, where we had just played the night before, the ceaseless touring should have tended to make the succeeding years into an indistinguishable blur but I have a cutting from the "Star" of January 1942 which refers to a very typical week in our life. We had played at Leicester, Warrington, Wigan and Blackpool, returning to London late on the Saturday night for a rehearsal and afternoon Sunday concert at the Albert Hall with Sydney Beer. He allowed me to conduct my own arrangement of some Rameau pieces: "Suite for Strings" after which, as the "Star" reporter put it: "Mr. Temple Savage returned to his usual place in the band." We then hurried out into the snow to catch a bus to Golders Green where we had just taken over the Orpheum for a new series of concerts. This first one was the "Messiah", I can't think when we rehearsed it, with Peter Pears and poor Isobel Baillie huddled in her fur coat most of the time in the unheated hall. No doubt we were off again on Monday; the problems of laundry were terrible!

The simple necessity of providing players, music and instruments all in the same place at the same time could become a herculean task when our efforts were pitted against the combined forces of enemy action, appalling weather and chronic disruption and delay on the railways. Once, in the depths of winter, music and instruments arrived safely at Preston but we were stuck in a train in the snow all night and only arrived in time to give the second of two scheduled concerts. Then we set off for Wakefield where we found the situation reversed; the music and instruments had been shunted off, no one quite knew where, and by the time they were located we could again give only the second of two concerts. One summer, after a concert in Birmingham, we were scheduled to play in the afternoon at St James' School, Malvern but once again music and instruments had vanished in the opposite direction. This time there was a happy ending, they were located by the resourceful stationmaster, the concert was postponed until the evening and at long last a little engine with one solitary truck full of instruments was seen puffing towards us in the golden light while the whole school gathered with us on the platform to welcome it.

Instruments were not my headache, the music was quite enough for me. It travelled with us in huge baskets known as skips and whenever we touched down in London I would hasten to the office in Regent Street to empty, sort and repack them for the next tour. I would know the programmes well in advance and on certain tours we might be playing the same programme in each town which simplified matters but we could need up to two weeks music with us. At first we had very little music of our own although we had the use of all Beecham's library. Other works would have to be hired from the relevant publishers. If it was from Boosey and Hawkes I had only to step downstairs into the hire library but if it should be from Goodwin and Tabb or Novello's someone would have to run to Dean Street or Wardour Street to organize it and there was never much time. I was buying in as much music as I could but anything that came from Teddy O'Brien was always part of a lot and I had to take odd things like overtures by Reinecke, long since forgotten, in order to get what I wanted. Then the Directors would query the bill, saying: "We'll never play that!" to which I would reply "You never know." By the time the office moved to Welbeck Street towards the end of the war we had quite a sizeable library which included various items that I had presented myself.

If I suddenly needed to hire anything when we were in the North I could call on Mr. Siddell and his daughter who had a vast hire library in a basement off the London Road in Manchester. I believe the BBC acquired it after his death. I know I had to dash over from Bolton once because the Grieg Piano Concerto had gone missing yet again – we never seemed to play anything else! Any other problems would have to be sorted out in shouted phone conversations over bad lines to Jocelyn in the office who was inclined to panic, (and who can blame her?) but generally managed to put something on a train for me. I remember being rudely awakened from a nap and hauled off the train at Grantham by the stationmaster with a message from Jocelyn to say that the "Enigma Variations" had been left behind and she had put them on the next train. I then had to use most of my week's wages on the hire of a car to transport me and the Variations across country to Oundle school for an afternoon concert.

In the hurry of packing an orchestral part could sometimes slip into another set and as most of the parts had standard covers it was not easily noticeable. We once arrived at Wolverhampton apparently without the first oboe part of the Overture to "Benevenuto Cellini" which we would be rehearsing that afternoon with Sargent. I always travelled with plenty of manuscript paper so I spent my entire lunch-hour frantically copying out the entire part – just finishing it in time. Sure enough, it turned up later with the parts of another piece we had recently played in the same programme. Most of our efforts to avoid disaster were successful but sometimes there was utterly nothing to be done as on the occasion of William Walton's Honorary Doctorate at Oxford.

We had come straight down to Oxford from the North without touching London and the orchestral parts of Walton's Violin Concerto which Henry Holst was to play on this auspicious occasion should have been already sent down from London for us. They had not arrived but there was plenty of time to phone Jocelyn and tell her to get on a train with them if necessary – only there happened to be an air-raid which once more knocked out the telephone exchange and it was quite impossible to contact London. It was obvious that Willy was bitterly disappointed and had gone out to get quietly drunk. I could see him sitting hiccupping gently during the concert in his doctoral robes while Henry Holst played the Brahms instead and we used parts borrowed from the University library.

Finally there was the dreadful day when the shit really hit the fan. We had been playing Ravel's "Schéhérezade" on several occasions but for some quite unfathomable reason it had not been repacked in the basket before we left London for York at the start of a new tour. We not only left without the parts but *with* seven percussion players engaged as extras just for that one piece. I had to break it to the Directors that these players would have nothing to do. Not one but seven players who would have to be paid just the same! Even after more than forty years it still makes my blood run cold. Later on, when I was caught up in the cross-fire of political in-fighting, this was quickly remembered as an excuse to get rid of me. Fortunately, by then I wanted to go!

· 16 ·

NATURALLY, conductors of stature like Sargent and Boult would always be in demand for autographs after a concert – Sir Adrian would charge half-a-crown and donate it to charity – but, believe it or not, unglamorous lot though we must have been in our ill-fitting dress-suits, badly-laundered shirts and – oh, horror – even some made-up ties, (though after my early training by Aileen I never sank to this) we too attracted a following of fans. They were usually very young girls, known as the Orchestra Popsies, who would cluster round the artists' entrance as we made one of our recurrent visits to their home town and offer to knit us sweaters. The tour known to us as the "Midland Blitz" would regularly involve Birmingham, Nottingham, Walsall and Wolverhampton and by 1944 Bristol, Leicester, Coventry and Watford were all visited at least once a month, so the girls did not have too long to wait for the return of their idols. Indeed, Bristol became the orchestra's second home and I had good friends there, Sylvia and Jex Woods, with whom I could stay. Those among us who adopted the naval lifestyle of a wife in every port, openly encouraged by Russell who did not at that time approve of marriage though he settled for it later, found it easy to pick up the threads of their various liaisons on return visits and there was one trumpet player who was reputed to have two perfectly-organized families, one in London and one in St. Ives, Huntingdon.

It seemed to be the string players who were the most sought after – the tradition of the romantic, long-haired Paganini-style violinist obviously died hard. The leader of the second fiddles, Reg Boothroyd, was particularly successful with the ladies, which was surprising as he was very lethargic, but he did not seem to manage matters very well and when we returned to London his wife would appear at the stage door to sort him out. The most popular without a doubt was Jean

90

Pougnet, the leader who succeeded Thomas Matthews. He had been a member of a brilliant string quartet at the Academy just before the war, in which Hugo Rignold was the viola, but they had all decided to join Jack Hylton and so their repertoire at first was largely dance music. His new job with us meant an incredible amount of work for him. In 1942 Henry Wood had at last invited us to the Proms, having held out for a long time because of our connection with Beecham, and the concerts required a vast repertoire. At Prom rehearsals the standard works were generally taken as read so when Pougnet asked Basil Cameron if we could rehearse a few passages of Tschaikowsky's Fifth Symphony: "Oh, I don't think you need worry about that," says Basil. "That work always goes well."

"Yes, I know," replied poor Jean, "but I've never played it before!" There was no problem; he was an impeccable player, a perfectionist who practised for hours on end and nearly drove me insane one afternoon in Oxford. I was preparing the music for the evening and Jean in the leader's room next door practised one solitary note for the entire afternoon. Perhaps his French name added to his glamour but he was in any case tall, well-built and handsome with thick fair hair. His fans were many and devoted, two little Waafs in particular would hitch-hike from town to town in pursuit of him, and at times he would try to persuade any of us who were free to take a few of them off his hands.

If we were not keen on squiring the Popsies and had seen all the local films some of us would go for energetic walks or even rowing on Loch Lomond on the Scottish tours, form poker schools or buy Hugo grammars and try to learn another language – I remember tackling both German and Dutch while the same Percy Frosdick who had frightened the waiter in Berlin in 1936 by announcing that he was a vegetable was still struggling away to acquire a foreign tongue with a notable lack of success. Sometimes out of sheer boredom one might have a shouting-match with a colleague. My good friend Francis Bradley (third horn and one of the directors) and I had a regular stand-up row about once a year which frightened everybody but ourselves. It was generally about something quite unimportant like the seating of the orchestra or whether Southend was an awful place or not and we forgot about it immediately afterwards.

There were, as well, frequent letters to be written organizing one's temporary addresses well in advance though, looking back, it seems to me that I was generally fortunate in finding somewhere to lay my head and was never reduced to the straits of Michael Dobson, the first oboe, who once had to spend the whole night on a bench at New Street Station, Birmingham. My worst experience was a night spent three in a bed in Swansea with Francis Bradley and Charlie Gregory when my system of forward planning had for once broken down completely. I had to organize my permanent accommodation as well for Hilda was living in a house we had bought in Watford, most of her work being at the School of Music there, and even had I particularly wanted to, it was impossibly difficult to get back there between tours so by 1943 I was living in bachelor digs in Kilburn for the Prom season and then Leonard Fleming, the fourth horn, introduced me to the home of Lucy and Victor Brightmore at 17, Addison Gardens, Kensington where various musicians lodged in great comfort.

It must have been at about the same time that I heard of my first love, Aileen, again from an old Wimbledon acquaintance, and very tragic news it was. Her husband, Frank Rendall, having surivived many sorties as bomber navigator, had been knocked down by a car and killed when crossing the road to come on leave. Aileen had apparently taken up spiritualism in her inability to accept his death. I went at once to her parents' home in Oxshott but only managed to see her sister, Aileen was out at a séance. We did meet again not long afterwards, I found her just as she had always been except that, while enjoying her company, I was no longer under her spell. She talked ceaselessly about spiritualism and the need to "get in touch" but, like all her enthusiasms, it was both violent and short-lived. She soon vanished again to live on a farm in Essex with an odd and taciturn character who had been at school with me and played the flute in the school orchestra. I suppose I must have known his first name once but only remember him as "Tew". What their relationship was I never quite understood but I had long ago stopped trying to work out the motives for Aileen's behaviour. She would reappear in London from time to time and we would meet, not finally breaking contact until 1947 after some curious events which I will come to in due course.

It was in 1943 also that my mother, who had been ailing for some years, died of cancer in a nature-cure nursing home run by a friend of my father's outside Hereford. I was in Manchester when I received the telegram from my father and, being distraught, jumped on the first train without pausing to think that it was too late, it was already all over. I ended up in Hereford at two o'clock in the morning with no means of getting out to the nursing home until daylight. In despair, I went to the police station and begged them to put me in a cell. The sergeant was sorry, they were all full, but he took pity on me and let me into the empty Town Hall, all laid out with row upon row of mattresses in case a blitz on Birmingham should lead to large-scale evacuation, and there I spent a lonely and desolate night.

It was really the accommodation problem that led me in 1943 to compose the only original work of mine ever to be performed in public (at the London Philharmonic Arts Club in Charing Cross Road in 1946). I was as usual busy copying and my hotel had no convenient long table so I had taken to going down to Colston Hall during the day where I could find one to my liking. A strange assortment of instrumentalists seemed to be practising there: a trumpet (Malcolm Arnold), a flute (Richard Adeney), a viola (Wrayburn Glasspool) and a bassoon (George Alexandra). My exasperation at this odd combination led me to compose "Five Foolish Fancies" for them, entitled "On Tour" and comprising an "Overture to a Reluctant Landlady", a limping March, "Looking for Digs", a Waltz, "No Rehearsal" and a Dirge, "No Beer". The fifth number has passed from my recollection and the score has long been lost. I was more successful as an arranger and on December 28th 1943 the orchestra performed my transcription of Handel's B minor Oboe Sonata for full orchestra at Colston Hall and the Press were gracious. The effect was "fully successful", I had "captured the true Handelian spirit" and "we shall doubtless be hearing this work again". Of course we didn't – except for one solitary broadcast by the BBC Northern Orchestra one Boxing Day. I even managed to lose the recording someone made of it for me!

My piece had been conducted by Vilem Tausky, a most engaging and colourful musical personality who generally wore his uniform as a member of the Free Czech Forces when on the rostrum; but at about that time we were experimenting with the appointment of a Musical Director for a year, Anatole Fistoulari, a Russian by birth. He had, unfortunately, a very limited repertoire and was reluctant to enlarge it though we did manage to get him to learn Mahler's Fourth Symphony. He had some incentive for that as his wife was Mahler's daughter. We were criticized, of course, for not appointing a British conductor and the experiment was not repeated.

I have a cutting from a Bristol paper with a review of a 1944 concert under Fistoulari which certainly gives the impression that we were beginning to show signs of wear and tear although the reviewer does his utmost to be rapturous whenever he can. "Although not at its best during parts of the performance what it (the orchestra) gave was good to listen to." In Rossini's "Semiramide" overture: "the pitch of the orchestra was varied and most of the accents were not always correctly placed." Oh dear. The Cesar Franck Symphony in D minor was "brilliantly and expressively played – only just lacking in that super-finish which . . ." Enough said. But what does he expect after nearly five years of seven days a week on tea and buns? "One thing noticeable was the beautiful tone quality of the bass clarionet (R. Temple Savage.)" Well, thank goodness for that though it does sound rather like the one-eyed man being king in the country of the blind. The same notice announces – could it be with relief? – the imminent return of Sir Thomas Beecham from America and a concert under his baton for November 29.

ALTHOUGH the year with Fistoulari was not totally successful the idea behind it, that the orchestra was suffering from the lack of a unifying hand, was a sound one. We had toured not only with Sargent, Boult, Cameron and Charles Hambourg but also with Edric Cundell, Warwick Braithwaite, Richard Tauber, Constant Lambert and two experienced Kapellmeister, Heinz Unger and Karl Rankl, able to take on anything at the shortest notice, but all this did not add up to a style and I think we all hoped for great things from Beecham's return.

I mentioned earlier that Constant Lambert, brilliant though he was, was really at his best as a ballet conductor; to put it bluntly, he was incapable of following a singer or instrumentalist in a rubato. Jean Pougnet liked to play as encores little Kreisler "lollipops" which I would orchestrate for him and we had to abandon one of these, "Schöne Rosmarin", entirely because Lambert could not manage to follow Pougnet. He was particularly fond of light French music, reacted against the whole German tradition and thought a composer like Dvořak quite appalling. Nevertheless the Directors put him down to conduct Dvořak's cello concerto and between his dislike of the music and his difficulty in accompanying the soloist we had all the ingredients for a disaster.

Richard Tauber was as talented a conductor as he was a singer; his repertory included a great deal of Schubert and was, like Fistoulari's, limited. He was the most charming, genial person, addressing everyone indscriminately as "Schnappelapumpi" which I think must be the Viennese equivalent of "Thingumajig", and often inviting a few of us back to his hotel after concerts to regale us with drink and stories. He was a great film buff and in his young days in Dresden had particularly liked to sing the role of Narraboth in "Salome" because he would be killed after twenty minutes and could catch the last show at the picture-house. Imagine his rage and frustration when one night the guards forgot to drag him off and he had to spend another hour and a half flat on his face on stage!

It is perhaps not surprising that by now I felt myself able to express publicly a few of my views on conducting and the exponents of the art. We always liked visiting Nottingham where the girls all seemed pretty and the audiences were very appreciative so that we could do something more than our bread-and-butter programmes; so it was here that I launched out into public speaking with a talk to the Nottingham Music Club on conducting. The local paper reported that I announced firmly: "There is far too much adulation of the conductor today" and went on to refer scathingly to those who worked on the method of "What can I do with this piece?" instead of "What did the composer have in mind?" At that time, according to the press cutting, although Weingartner was already firmly on his pedestal, Bruno Walter was my particular idol. I know that I had been very impressed when I played Mahler under his baton when he first came over from Austria after the Anschluss, and his Mozart had a wonderful singing quality. Trying to remember now when he left my own private group of giants, I recall that I found it impossible to read his autobiography because of his unshakable belief there could be no correct opinion but his own, and also that he seemed much changed when he eventually returned to England from the States, his manner to the orchestra having taken on the bullying quality that seems to be accepted and even expected by orchestras over there. This produced reservations in my appreciation of him – my choices are entirely personal and subjective.

For my talk to the Nottingham Music Club the records were put on the turn-table by Denys Potts, a very young man hardly out of his teens, the son of the Vicar of Ruddington; I was drawn to him at once by his air of gentle and genuine interest in anything one said to him. He was working for Rolls Royce at the time, at Skipton where he had started a gramophone club and he asked me to give my talk again for his members. He was shortly to go up to Oxford to read engineering and from there he called upon me to perform yet again, this time in rooms in one of the colleges where, at 9.25 pm, the lecture had to stop while the ladies in the audience were escorted to the gate. I did not know that various musical big-wigs were among those present, including the composer, Egon Wellesz, who gave a loud snort of laughter when I made my usual reference to most English conductors having descended from the organ loft, and Sir Thomas Armstrong and Dr. Sidney Watson who, having reached the rostrum by this very route, gave a snort of a less approving nature.

There is no doubt that Oxford was my friend Denys's spiritual home but his choice of course had been totally mistaken. Quite undeterred by his failure at engineering, he turned to modern languages, took his degree in French and went on from strength to strength until he became Head of French at Keble College where he is today. This is one of the happiest examples that I have met of someone able to realize where his real talent lies in time to make a success of his life after a false start, instead of perpetually bewailing what might have been.

My other extra-mural activity at this time was certainly of more general interest. Boosey and Hawkes numbered among their staff three distinguished refugees, music editors and publishers who had left Austria after the Anschluss: Alfred Kalmus, Ernst Roth and Erwin Stein. They started a series of Boosey and Hawkes concerts; Erwin Stein had been a pupil of Schoenberg and the first concert, in the Aeolian Hall in 1942, consisted of Schoenberg's "Pierrot Lunaire" (the first performance in England for a very long time) and Walton's "Façade". I was one of the players approached by Alfred Kalmus, who was managing the concerts, and we rehearsed for nine whole months. Every time I was in London I had to go to Regent Street for interminable instructions from Irwin Stein who was to conduct the Schoenberg. This involved advice on the way to play more or less every note. Such intensive coaching was totally alien to the British players' approach; we were by tradition brilliant and professional sight-readers, last-minute men who were expected not only to tackle everything put before us but also to give a performance. I had learned in my early days that it was not done to ask for the part to practise! Whereas the Vienna Philharmonic might have the parts of "Arabella" six months before the first performance, in England in the early nineteen hundreds the tradition had been one of "bums on seats" – as long as somebody played it didn't matter if it was the principal or a deputy. One would do a rehearsal or the concert but not necessarily both and Sir Henry Wood formed his own orchestra to try to do away with this practice but many players still cling to it and broke away from him to form the London Symphony Orchestra. Although this pernicious habit had died out, a high sight-reading ability was still obligatory as rehearsal time for British orchestras was so inadequate. Different methods suit different national temperaments and the hyper-meticulous preparation of Erwin Stein, much thought I liked him, was entirely irksome to a British instrumentalist.

Our last rehearsal was held in the British Museum as the violinist, Dea Gombrich, was the wife of the Director. I was by then in sullen and unco-operative mood after nine months of rehearsal and I played one movement of "Pierrot Lunaire" a semitone out on the A clarinet instead of the B flat, just to see if anyone would notice. Nobody did but Erwin Stein was very, very upset when I confessed although much laughter was heard in many other quarters in London and when we went for our next film session (we played for various Ministry of Information propaganda films) I found that K. Ernest Irving had heard all about it.

Walton conducted "Façade" from behind a replica of the screen used at the first performance in the twenties while the verse was excellently spoken by Constant Lambert; when we recorded it later it was divided between Dame Edith and Peter Pears. The cellist was a very serious refugee lady who was extremely good at the Schoenberg but did not manage too well sight-reading the Walton. Willy said that what he really wanted was "a good hack cellist" and I thoughtlessly suggested George Walton as he could play anything. He was duly engaged but somehow the dreadful phrase "hack cellist" got back to him – there are always people about waiting to repeat what should never be repeated – and neither he nor any member of his family would speak to me afterwards for having thought of him in such a connection. However, the concert was a tremendous success and there was a big party afterwards at which Willy at the piano was doing some very naughty impersonations, notably of Peter Pears singing Britten songs. I don't think Walton and Britten ever got on very well, they were so utterly different. I went to have a drink with both of them during the 1945 Cheltenham Festival at which the "Sea Interludes" from "Peter Grimes" had been given for the first time (the opera had just had its first performance) and I was very conscious of the tension between them in every casual remark.

· 18 ·

IT WAS fortunate that our first visitors from abroad after the Liberation were all very fine conductors, after the rather lean fare of the past few years they brought a breath of fresh air. Charles Münch, from Alsace, was perhaps the most exciting in performance but, although the Swiss Ernest Ansermet, was an intellectual and his approach mathematical, his results were never dry. In any case a mathematical approach is what you need for "Petrouchka" (which, I mentioned earlier, we recorded with him) because of the rhythmic complications. Unfortunately Tom Russell did not allow conductors to choose their own programmes and some of them, especially Münch, were given totally inappropriate selections, one concert including a Souza March, Ravel's "Bolero" and a Tschaikowsky Symphony. Latterly, a programme committee was formed, all part of the co-operative image. I was on it but was totally frustrated; most players had no idea of constructing a programme, bearing in mind the different keys in which the works are written. One dreadful programme was made up almost entirely of works in D major which would have meant an evening of monotony with the exception of one little piece in E flat in the middle – which would have the effect of a sudden unpleasant shock. The Italian Victor de Sabata sent over a whole selection of balanced programmes before his visit and the committee took one work from each in a meaningless hotch-potch.

All in all, the whole concept of the dedicated band of brothers had gone a little sour. I was in trouble again for sending a postcard to Walton suggesting he might like to look in on Albert Coates' rehearsal of his First Symphony in case things were not to his liking; he duly arrived and made a few mild comments but I received a dressing-down from Russell for "disloyalty". I could not see this – it seemed only right to me that a composer should have the opportunity of attending a rehearsal of his own work. Players could also be heard grumbling that they would like a day or two off and – unheard-of boldness – what about a holiday? Various projects for involving the players in every kind of decision were not at all successful. Besides the programme committee there was also a committee to decide which of the various test records was the one to be issued after a recording session, a crazy idea if ever there was one. We were not in the least qualified to judge, this must be for the conductor, but by that time one had begun to feel that, for ideological reasons, Russell would have preferred to have no conductor at all — as in Russia for a short time after the Revolution.

Of course Beecham did indeed return and everything was laid on for him – the best hotels and even Government permission for a chauffeur-driven limousine to take him everywhere. A tour was arranged and the first rehearsal was at Wembley Town Hall. Dear old Berta Geissmar, who had cared for his library, watched his interests devotedly and kept his name before the public for four years by little paragraphs in the papers, was with us eagerly awaiting him. He arrived an hour and a half late (by which time the orchestra was very restive) with his new wife, Betty Humby-Beecham, and ignored poor Berta completely. I think it broke her heart.

At first, those of us who knew him felt great delight at playing for him once more, but the orchestra was full of new faces and Beecham always needed players who understood him. The magic did not seem to work any more and there were constant niggles. The tours were a great success and we made records with him again but nothing could ever be as it had been and I cannot help feeling that Russell was the last person to deal tactfully with Beecham's idiosyncrasies. Our relationship shrivelled slowly until by 1946 it was dead and Beecham had left us to form his own orchestra, the Royal Philharmonic.

I did, nevertheless, have one final pleasant evening with him not long after his return when he was staying at St. John's Wood with Betty Humby-Beecham's parents. He was preparing one of his many Handel Suites – the "Faithful Shepherd", and wanted me to go over one evening to help him mark up the parts. We didn't do much work, he sent his wife off to bed and we drank and talked late into the night. Suddenly it occurred to him that perhaps I had not dined but, accustomed as he was to ring for room service, he was rather at a loss and trotted off to the kitchen, returning after some time with two small sweet biscuits on a plate. By the time I finally left I was absolutely ravenous, all public transport had shut down for the night and I had to take a very expensive taxi.

In view of the cruel ingratitude of the treatment Geissmar had received from Beecham I was particularly glad on VE Day 1945 to keep a long-standing promise I had made to her. In the worst days of the blitzes I used to say to her: "Never mind, Berta, when we win the war I'll take you out to lunch" and I duly took her to Gennaro's (where the ladies were always given a flower) and ordered a modest bottle of wine. She was always very insecure, conscious of the fact that she was German as well as Jewish, and I reminded her that she belonged to England now. I was touched to discover later that this little occasion had meant a great deal to her and she refers to it at the end of her book "The Baton and the Jackboot" – and to me as "original and lovable" which my wife unkindly said made me sound like a new line in teddy bears but which I appreciated none the less.

In November we were all off to Paris, Brussels and Antwerp, the first artists to tour in Europe since the end of hostilities. We travelled to Newhaven from Victoria, arriving late in the evening and were immediately herded on to our boat and left to fend for ourselves overnight, sleeping on any available deckchair or even on the deck itself, until we sailed next morning. I never understood the reason behind this, probably just lack of planning, but one accepted all discomforts quite meekly then. When we arrived in Paris we were taken to the Gare de l'Est and lodged in a series of *wagons-lits* opposite a disused platform with access to the very unhygienic station facilities (all *à la turque*, of course,) while Beecham lodged in style at the Ritz. I accompanied Adolf Borsdorf when he went to pay Beecham's bill, it was very sizeable.

At least in our train we had a compartment each and we were like children on holiday, sightseeing endlessly, always on foot as the Americans had all the taxis and well provided with cigarettes which were the most acceptable form of tip anywhere. Some of us went to Versailles, Notre Dame, the Louvre and the Opéra while others, it is said, went in search of "Le Sphinxe" a famous brothel of the time. I saw Berlioz' "Damnation of Faust" at the Opéra – at least, I could see very little of the stage but I had a fine bird's-eye view of two trombone players who seemed to be having a fiery political argument whenever they had a few bars' rest. At one point they even left the pit, presumably to settle their differences once and for all. It was

November 11th when I went to "Pelléas et Mélisande" at the Opéra Comique and at the end of the first act a short, stout official in a tricolor sash suddenly marched on stage, positioned himself between the two principal singers and proceeded to harangue us in a fervent Gallic manner which I am afraid the English visitors found very hard to take.

I visited the elegant showrooms of Durand et Cie near the Madeleine and bought scores of Dukas' "Ariane et Barbe Bleue" and Ravel's "L'Heure Espagnole" and went to Buffet's to order myself a new E flat clarinet. I was supposed to play the E flat clarinet in Britten's "Sea Interludes" but my good instrument had been stolen from the Albert Hall a couple of years earlier and the American replacement which was all I could get in war-time was quite terrible. I was forced to transpose the part on my C clarinet so it seemed the right moment to order a good instrument. The currency problem was solved by the kindness of Charles Münch who paid for it in francs which I would reimburse in pounds on his next visit to England. When it was ready the clarinet was smuggled over in the diplomatic bag; I had to collect it from the Arts Council and be rebuked by John Denison.

We gave our Paris concerts in the Théâtre des Champs Elysées, Münch conducting the last one; the place was packed and everything was received with wild enthusiasm, even the Britten "Sea Interludes" from "Peter Grimes" which were probably not much to the French taste and which Beecham did not know and had not wanted to conduct – rudely referring to the "Bugger's Opera" in a Press conference – but he was eventually over-persuaded by the directors.

There was no train in a railway siding for us in Brussels but the good old Hotel Métropole just as before in 1935, even the food seemed moderately good compared with Paris, but the streets seemed curiously full of girls with large baskets, presumably from the country districts, calling their wares: "Sandwichs, sandwichs!" huge chunks of crusty bread which they were selling to the hungry townspeople. In Antwerp our concert was in a magnificent old theatre with the most wonderful acoustics but which seemed to be constructed entirely of wood; I could not stop thinking of the frightful fire hazard and looking round for the nearest exit. Then we were on our way home again, enduring a very rough crossing indeed. I have a photo showing us all in our life-jackets with myself in the back row wearing a very pained expression and about to bolt for the side any minute.

· 19 ·

BACK in London, among the old friends beginning to appear to play with us again was Tony Baines on the contra-bassoon. He had been a prisoner of war in Italy and had escaped when he was about to be transferred to Germany. He told me how he spent some time hiding in the countryside, smoking spinach as he could get no tobacco and befriended by a village priest with whom he spent some happy hours singing extracts from "Tosca" accompanied on the church organ. Sadly, he was recaptured but promptly set about organizing an orchestra in his German POW camp where he found a record of Rimsky-Korsakov's "Scheherezade" and, incredibly, made a score and parts from it – he had a wonderful "inner ear". He then obtained instruments through the Red Cross and taught them to his fellow-inmates! He was now in a comfortable job as Hospitals Education Officer in an office in Curzon Street and had just collected another ad hoc group of players from among the local Education Corps personnel. This "London District Orchestra" was to give a concert and he suggested that I might like to come. It is strange that of all the hundreds of programmes I must have played or listened to I should remember so clearly that this one consisted of a Bach Suite, Dvořak's First Symphony and the Ballet Music from "Faust". Perhaps it is because it was quite diabolical – or perhaps because of subsequent events. Anyway, the audience of distinguished-looking Education colonels and the like were looking mildly astonished, as well they might; Tony, of course, was enjoying himself hugely in his usual unselfconscious way. As soon as I could I slipped quietly out to the nearby "Antelope" just off Piccadilly and a curious thing occurred.

I was not to meet Valerie until some weeks later and neither of us realized until much later that we had in fact seen and noticed each other for the first time that evening. She was working in the same office

103

as Tony and came into the "Antelope" with him after the concert. She saw me at once, so she says, sitting on a bar stool with my back to the bar, wearing a green checked shirt and looking very bored. Without knowing why, she immediately asked Tony: "Who is that man?" but did not remember his reply, except that she had an idea that I was someone important. She knows that she was being consciously vivacious during the evening, rather hoping to tempt me to join the group, but she did not turn round. I, for my part, remember seeing a very slim ATS officer with her long hair rolled up round a ribbon in war-time fashion and wandering over to the fringes of their group, also vaguely in the hope of an introduction but nothing came of it.

It was not until New Year's Eve 1945 that Tony brought her with him again, this time to the "Norfolk" in Paddington. After rather a drunken evening which had started as a foursome and during which Tony in his Bohemian fashion had wanted us all to go back to spend the night on the floor of his digs but Valerie had demurred (because, she confessed to me afterwards, she was wearing such unattractive Army issue underwear), I saw her back to her ATS quarters in Sloane Square. I stopped at a convenient advertisement for our next Sunday concert at the Stoll Theatre, in the Underground station, and asked her if she would like to come. She came – and everything began to change for me.

At first we were faced with innumerable problems: I was still married to Hilda and divorces were taking up to two years, the backlog of cases was so great; Valerie was still engaged to an Army officer in India; she was demobbed in March 1946 and had to return home to Parbrook in Somerset, a place so remote that whenever I tried to phone her the operator would insist at first that the exchange did not exist; her family were strongly protective and her elder sister and her husband wished to meet me and assess my suitability and prospects – and my position with the LPO had become very insecure. Thomas Russell was away, recovering from his T.B. and the devious Charlie Gregory was having it all his own way. He told me without any preliminaries that they had appointed Jack Jones (father of Philip Jones, the trumpet player) as Librarian as they considered that the job should no longer be combined with that of a player. I had been a possible suitor at £15 a week but the bass clarinet alone was not going to provide for the costs of a divorce and setting up a new home.

The appointment of Karl Rankl as Musical Director of the Royal

Opera House had just been announced and I told him of my longing to return there permanently; he promised to do his best for me. Not unnaturally I have a continuing sense of loyalty to the man who realized my dearest wish but in any case at that time I only knew him as a lively, friendly little man with a sense of humour, a hatred of what he called "scratching your left ear with your right hand" and a fondness for outrageous statements like: "Of course, Beethoven is a very second-rate composer." It was not until he had been stretched beyond his capacity and endurance that he became the frightening hysteric we were later to see. Youngest son of a huge Austrian peasant family, pupil of Schoenberg, musical director of Graz Opera house, himself a prolific composer, he was the only person then immediately available with the knowledge and experience of running a repertory Opera House. In the long rum it was not, after all, what the powers that be really wanted; they dreamed of the big international stars and the old style of grand opera at Covent Garden. Opera in English with an integrated company of British singers may have been the foundation they planned at first to build on but the flimsy structure could not last and Rankl with his provincial opera house criteria would fall with it.

By the time Russell returned I had already been interviewed by David Webster, the General Administrator, and offered the job of Librarian and bass clarinet at £21 a week, (the orchestra then earned £18) for this I had to play at least three times a week before earning any overtime. I had no written contract with the LPO but such was the strength of Russell's hold over us that I remembered being quite anxious lest he should in some way prevent me from leaving and we still keep the telegram I sent to Valerie when all was safely agreed, with a few reservations as to engagements to be fulfilled before I finally departed.

The next problem to be tackled was the divorce; in those days it was still a matter of distasteful evidence from hotel chambermaids and I was glad of Aileen's offer to have us to stay at her farm in Essex in order to provide the necessary evidence. We spent a few summer days there, incongruously surrounded by her collection of oriental masks and weapons and sleeping in a vast carved bed that had been a four poster but had been decapitated in order to force it into the little farmhouse. We were rather surprised to find Aileen in the throes of a passionate affair with a very young, very thick German prisoner called Gerhard who sat open-mouthed while, in between cooking vast mounds of cabbage and potatoes for the farm-workers, she rendered Schubert's "Shepherd on the Rock" at the piano, a dish-cloth over her shoulder. All the same, everything appeared to go off amicably and it was not until months later when we had become desperate at the lack of progress in the case that we took a train to the solicitors in Watford. We discovered that when their clerk had called at Canney Farm for the evidence Aileen had refused to give it, saying that it would give her house a bad name, which, in view of the goings-on with the German prisoner we found doubly infuriating. We could only assume that she found the prospect of losing even one of her former worshippers unendurable; but Valerie was more a match even for Aileen. She simply turned to the lawyers and asked if, when the time came, she could give evidence herself, a more courageous act thirty-eight years ago than it may appear today; they were as astonished as they were relieved. So that was settled and now we had only to wait patiently. Undeterred, Aileen wrote to me again after I was married, wanting me to get in touch with her on some excuse or other but by then I felt she had really done enough damage and did not reply.

Part Three

THE ROYAL
OPERA HOUSE AGAIN
1946–63

· 20 ·

SHORTLY before I was due to take up my new appointment I received a little note from Sir Adrian Boult, wanting to know what had become of me and asking me to phone him. He had found time in the midst of all his commitments to be concerned about my welfare, having heard that I had left the LPO and thinking that I might be in difficulties. Valerie had escaped from Somerset by now and we both went to lunch with him and I was able to reassure him that I was not going to be on the bread-line. He unwittingly played the role of Good Fairy yet again when I was negotiating for a new bedsitter in a handsome double-fronted house, 36 Holland Villas Road, W.14, where there was also a basement flat which had been used as an air raid shelter but not yet been renovated; we had our eyes on it as a possible future home. Phyl and Eliot Bolton were to be good friends and kind landlords but during our interview we were perhaps over-eager, Phyl became cautious and began to hedge and murmur about references. My mind was a total blank – who could possibly be persuaded to give me a reference? – but Valerie decided that the moment was ripe for the odious practice of name-dropping and, with a surreptitious wink at me, said brightly: "Oh, I'm sure Sir Adrian would help, darling!" and somehow we found Phyl had become quite amenable and we never had to trouble Sir Adrian after all. I got the bed-sitter and a year later we were to move into the flat just as we had hoped.

I started work at the Opera House on a Tuesday, October 1st 1946, as I had to move to Holland Villas Road on the Monday – the removal men groaning theatrically: "Cor! ain't learning 'eavy?" as they shifted my scores. For this I was duly docked a day's pay which for some reason rankled with me for years and I always intended to ask for it when I retired, only I lost my nerve in the end. There was an atmosphere of beginning-of-term excitement and apprehension as there were not only dozens of new faces but many of us were new to the actual job we were now to do. Of the music staff only the invaluable Norman Feasey had been in the Opera House before the war and probably only Peter Gellhorn* had previously worked with an opera company. There was Eric Mitchell, just out of the Navy, always in black coat and striped trousers, squiring the tall, blonde mezzo-soprano, Constance Shacklock in her large picture hats – they were to marry within the year. There was the young composer, John Gardner with his great Beethoven-like head and there was the very, very well-connected Edward Renton – who was also an excellent repetiteur. I am afraid, though, that he will be chiefly remembered as the conductor of whom Robert Helpmann, on a ballet tour at Croydon, was to ask indignantly after trying to leap up and down to his slow tempi: "Have you never heard of gravity?" The chorus master was Douglas Robinson, down from Leeds and the splendid singing of the new opera chorus was perhaps the only unqualified success when the season opened. The stage doorkeeper was still the formidable Tom Jackson and I was also glad to see Norman-the-electrician whom I had loved to watch in the old days as he nonchalantly pulled on a pair of rubber gloves and, holding two live arc-carbons, one in each hand, brought them together for a mighty flash of lightning at the end of "Don Giovanni". In the orchestra there were only Frank Stead, Charlie Turner the percussion player and myself from the old LPO though others would reappear later, and I said I was far too busy being a librarian to be able to play for some time. In the end Joseph Shadwick, the leader, got tired of waiting and sent me in to play the "Rake's Progress" ballet at short notice.

I must admit I viewed my new job with great trepidation. I had never had to deal with so many different things, nor had such great responsibility. Also I was not used to the idea of an office-based existence but on my first day I found that no one had even thought of allocating a room to me anyway and I ended up sharing with the Assistant House Manager, a state of affairs that really could not continue. Soon I was settled under the stage in a little cell next to Fred Laurence's old office which I coveted as it had all the necessary shelving but which was occupied by the orchestra leader. It must have been the end of the first season before I managed to acquire it. Valerie

*Later Chorus Master at Glyndebourne and Director of the BBC Chorus

110

kept assuring me that if I had an In-tray and an Out-tray and worked from one to the other all would be well but I never really took to the idea.

When my telephone rang for the first time it was David Webster's secretary, Miss Kerr, to tell me that I had to obtain an import licence for the orchestral parts of "Coppelia" which Sadlers Wells Ballet were about to produce.

"How do I go about that?" I asked, hoping for clear instructions from this very efficient person.

"I've no idea," she said calmly. "You'll have to find out." So I put my copy of the "Times" in my In-tray and went off to find out by the simple process of asking everywhere until I came up with the answer. (I think it was the Post Office in the end.) Over the ensuing years I built up by this method a very considerable stock of answers until in the end people were asking me the questions, which was rather gratifying.

The San Carlo Opera Company of Naples were performing in the theatre at that time; I was not responsible for them in any way but occasionally I was approached for orchestral material to be used at their various recording sessions. In this way I made my first acquaintance with the vast, shadowy music-store under the stalls where huge parcels of scores and parts, tied up in black oilcloth reposed on slatted wooden shelves gathering thick black dust. (Incidentally, some insensitive person had actually suggested this grimy, airless dungeon as a possible place for me to work!) Material for a good number of the standard works was there, some of it nearly a hundred years old, the parts of Verdi's "I Masnadieri" having been well scorched in the last fire of 1852 – and a large quantity of very old pantomime music. We had played from much of the material before the war but it was not realistic to expect a new young generation of players to cope with such parts; the key signature was only given at the beginning of the act, or when it actually happened to change, so that when you turned over a page you could well forget what key you were in. Also the semi-quaver rests were indicated by a peculiar sign rather like the Prince of Wales' feathers, known as "butterfly rests" which could prove totally disconcerting to the uninitiated. Gradually, I worked to copy new sets of parts for several operas as they came into the repertory.

The vocal scores presented even more problems, there were never enough of them to go round for all the new singers joining the

111

company (in pre-war days the soloists brought their own) as well as the producer, the prompter, the lighting department, all the repetiteurs concerned and sometimes even the wardrobe. Further stocks were very hard to obtain; the RAF had flattened Ricordi's in Milan, Breitkopf were in Leipzig in East Germany – we were forced to scour the second-hand shops and even to advertise. Then there was the new rule that everything had to be sung in English which meant that, if we had not enough scores with an English translation, the words had to be written in by hand by anyone who wanted to earn a few pounds, and it was a very slow process. In view of the literary quality of most opera libretti you can imagine that it was also very, very boring. Sometimes the vocal scores had two languages in them already and then they had to be "stripped" – pasted over with thin slivers of white paper so there was room to write in the English version – not forgetting the addition or subtraction of a few notes here and there so it was all still singable.

At the very beginning my only official help was Charlie Stanley, an old gentleman in very poor health, armed with an insufflator, who had been brought in by Joe Shadwick to put out the music – and that is about all he did. After Christmas Valerie gave up her job teaching in a curious finishing school in Chelsea and arrived with her old portable typewriter to try to make some kind of amateur card-index of the contents of all those endless black bales. After being paid £5 for this she managed to stay on as general dogsbody at a minimum wage, pasting in cuts, writing in words, running errands and keeping up my morale, until we married in August 1947.

Our working conditions were not made easier by the ventilation system, which appeared to have been put in the wrong way round and blew quantities of dirt from the Market into our windowless cell, or by the frequent power cuts. During that first bitter post-war winter the electricity was only switched on in the daytime from noon to 2 p.m., otherwise one groped about below the stage with a torch or tried to commandeer a room with a window. I remember being very startled on opening one door to see a bald-headed, bearded figure fitfully illuminated in the gloom, hands apparently clasped in prayer before a great book. It was Geoffrey Corbett, the ballet conductor, studying his score and seated between the two great silver candlesticks which Tosca places at Scarpia's head at the end of the second act. He looked exactly like some mediaeval monk.

· 21 ·

WHATEVER the problems we had to get the season under way and as soon as I had sorted out the little matter of the import licence for "Coppelia" I went out again to lay in a large stock of manuscript paper on which to prepare a score of Purcell's "Fairy Queen", our opening production in January 1947 – Sadlers Wells Ballet were holding the fort until then. Constant Lambert had been commissioned to prepare the musical version of this hybrid work involving actors and dancers as well as singers and loosely based on "A Midsummer Night's Dream". Progress was slow; he did not bring me in much to work from and sometimes I even had to score passages myself from his verbal instructions. It also transpired later, when the bills began to come in, that he had farmed out a good deal of the work to others, in particular Professor Dent of Cambridge who scored several arias. When it was finally produced nobody liked it much apart from the beautiful *pas de deux* by Margot Fonteyn and Michael Somes as the Spirits of Air and Water and, of course, the magnificient choral singing; the soloists were all unmemorable.

After this we settled down to create a repertory: "Carmen", Massenet's "Manon", "Magic Flute", "Rosenkavalier", "Il Trovatore" and "Turandot". Most of the season's troubles seemed to involve those wretched English translations. There were two versions of "Carmen", one easily obtainable and the other almost impossible to find; of course they decided to do the latter. For "Manon" there was no English translation so Norman Feasey set to and made one which would be above all, easily singable – English being a notoriously ungrateful language in that respect. Everyone had a finger in the pie, every repetiteur altered words here and there as he coached the singers; in the end a whole committee of us were summoned to Rankl's room, armed with a vocal score each in order to try to make them all agree. And after all that the Press did not like the translation. For "Rosenkavalier" Alan Pryce-Jones had made a new English version which also began gradually to take on a rather different appearance as rehearsals progressed. When the author finally came to hear it he was rather annoyed and in the end a compromise version had to be submitted for his approval. Professor Dent had published translations of many of the standard works but they had never actually been fitted to the notes in a vocal score and this was an additional headache in the preparation of "Il Trovatore". The standard translation of "Turandot" was only in one or two old scores and "Magic Flute" was the only opera for which vocal scores with a printed translation were readily available. It was all a great deal of fuss about nothing as one still never heard much of the words anyway.

Edith Coates was our first Carmen and although she may have lacked some of the requirements for fascinating Don José she had an unerring dramatic instinct and the sinister quality of her voice as she saw death in the cards – John Gardner called it "the way she creeps up under the note" – sent shivers down one's spine. It was, however, at the very first orchestral rehearsal of the opera when, as Librarian, I had to be in attendance, that I noticed a complete change in Rankl's attitude to the players. He was no longer the genial, friendly little man I had known but aggressive, disagreeable – and he nagged. It was not the sort of atmosphere that English players would accept easily and at the end of the season there were many changes in the orchestra.

One can speculate endlessly on the causes of Rankl's behaviour but I cannot help feeling that an unstable domestic situation must have contributed to his growing hysteria. At a Christmas party at his home in St. John's Wood we had met a tall, impressive, tawny-haired woman with large, even, white teeth who had reminded us irresistibly of a lioness and who seemed to form part of the household. Later, when Karl and his wife came to dinner with us, Mrs. Rankl asked if she could bring her "adopted daughter" with her; so Christine came too and seemed, we thought, almost ostentatiously possessive towards Karl. Eventually she was to become the second Mrs. Rankl and cared for him devotedly in his later life but one shudders to think of poor Rankl with all his new responsibilities and the antagonism he was meeting, torn apart at home between the two women.

Constant Lambert was one of those most strongly antagonistic towards Rankl. He was one of the adjudicators for a prestigious competition for operatic composers held in 1947. Entries had to be submitted anonymously so I prepared a vocal score of the first act of Rankl's entry, "Deirdre of the Sorrows" from his rough sketches. It won one of the four prizes and Lambert was extremely put out when he discovered who the composer was! We had a private run-through of the first act at Rankl's house with David Franklin and other singers from the company but it was never publicly performed anywhere. Rafael Kubelik was supposed to be going to do it during his period as Musical Director in the fifties and I started to prepare the orchestral material at Rankl's request. Elsie Morrison, Kubelik's second wife would be the Deirdre. Nothing happened and eventually when I had the opportunity I privately asked Kubelik why it had all fallen through. He made a face and replied succinctly: "Politics." I know from other conversations as well that there were powerful people opposed to its performance.

For Massenet's "Manon" in 1947 we had a very young and pretty American soprano, Virginia McWatters, two household names – Heddle Nash and Dennis Noble – and a production by Frederick Ashton in which the balletic movements of the players fluttering their cards in the gambling scene in Act IV earned a spontaneous round of applause on the first night. I never ranked among the heads of department who were allotted free seats on these occasions but if I was not playing we would hire a car we could not afford from Adam and Eve Garage in Kensington and arrive in style with the rest. This first night had its agitating moments. The power cuts were still ruling our lives and there must have been one earlier in the evening. This meant that the solo on the Hammond organ which opens Act III, Scene II in Saint-Sulpice was very flat indeed and when the orchestra came in a startled Eric Mitchell had to transpose very quickly to get the rest of the piece to the same pitch. On stage too I felt something was wrong; Jess Walters as Des Grieux père was pacing up and down soliloquizing and I knew very well that by now he should be holding a conversation with his son. If it hadn't all been in English perhaps it would not have been so noticeable but anyway Heddle Nash finally came on at the double, having been caught by a jammed door in the lavatory. After all this we made sure that the Electricity Generating Board kept us forewarned about cuts – and no doubt the carpenter was sent to attend to the lavatory door.

Rankl did not want to use a prompter but Dennis Noble was taken ill and a cheerful baritone, George Hancock, who was rather a slow learner, had to take over the role of Lescaut at short notice. There was nothing for it but to open up the prompt box which had not been used since 1939 and was filled with dirt and spiders. It was also icy cold and Norman Feasey had to go out and buy a special anorak before taking up his position there. Operatic prompting is a difficult art, the singers are not given their notes, only the words and these must be given just before the end of the previous phrase or before their next entry. Some singers like to be prompted continously throughout the opera while others look at the prompter to indicate that they need help. In addition the prompter may have to point to various parts of the stage so the singer knows where to move next and I remember seeing the Italian prompters when the Scala came over, leaning right out of the prompt box with outstretched arms, pointing in all directions. Norman left nothing to chance with George Hancock, even placing pieces of paper on the furniture in strategic positions to assist him, rather like a treasure hunt.

We were expected to be able to play in any position within our section so I found myself as first clarinet for "Il Trovatore" under the baton of Rankl's assistant, Reginald Goodall. Since our College days I had only seen him occasionally when he was assisting Malcolm Sargent and had been repelled by his overt anti-semitism. He was by all accounts an excellent coach, singers loved to learn with him. A disciple of Furtwängler, his approach to conducting was intensely emotional which could produce fine moments if all was well but he had a very limited stick technique – openly despising such practical considerations – and so was unable to summon up or control such moments at will, in fact he was the antithesis of my ideal of a conductor. For example: anxious to start the Prelude to Act I of "La Traviata" pianissimo, he once produced such an imperceptible beat that we did not even notice it and he had to hiss indignantly to the orchestra: "I've started!" before he could make us react. His Wagner (*pace* Peter Heyworth!) must have been the slowest on record, it nearly stopped and, as Weingartner said, however slowly you play Wagner it must move. With Reggie one could begin to understand why Nietzsche said that Wagner's music had "the heartbeat of a slug". We really did fall out over the Dance of the Apprentices in "Meistersinger" when I was again playing first clarinet and he took it so slowly that my musical conscience refused to allow me to play it at that speed and I put down my instrument. After this we did not speak for years until we finally settled our differences over dinner in a hotel in Entebbe on our way back from Rhodesia in 1953.

Peter Gellhorn, Rankl's other assistant, conducted several performances of "Magic Flute" and I was again playing first clarinet. A beautiful and sensitive pianist, he was very knowledgeable and very hard-working; unlike Reggie Goodhall he had an excellent stick technique but nothing he could do as a conductor was ever right for the Press, perhaps because of his association with Rankl. In spite of this I can say confidently that I have played for many worse performances than those conducted by these two much-maligned men. I think that Peter's true problem stemmed from the fact that, on his own admission, he did not like to look directly at the players and so he had no real contact with us but was, as it were, conducting an ideal performance in his head or in a small space around him.

Probably the most successful production of our first year was "Turandot" with sets by Leslie Hurry and Dame Eva Turner in the title role. She was already in her middle fifties but her magnificent voice had lost none of its power and only a little of its sharpness of definition. Constant Lambert conducted and before the first night the tenor, Walter Midgley, came down to see me and asked me to mark various pauses he intended to make very clearly in the score so Lambert could not miss them.

"Is he still having trouble following singers, then?" I asked innocently.

"Follow?" cried Midgley in his curiously high voice, "He couldn't follow an open bottle of Chanel down Piccadilly on a hot night!"

After the end of the season we were all to go on tour for six weeks without any extra money as the Union considered that we were so highly paid it was not necessary. My attention at the time was chiefly concentrated on the question of whether we would be able to get married before this. Incredibly, my divorce case at last came up at the very beginning of July, the decree absolute would be through on August 15th, we would get married on Saturday August 16th while someone else packed up the music for the tour for me – and on Sunday August 17th we would travel to Glasgow, of all places to spend a honeymoon, where the tour was to start.

· 22 ·

IT WAS 92° in the shade as I scurried across Waterloo station to catch my train to Woking. Matters were not helped by my suit which had been tailored for me in an excellent but rather warm cloth and my face must have matched the crimson rose that my father had brought from his garden for my buttonhole. A voice hailed me and whom should I see but Sir Adrian Boult smiling and saying: "Why, Mr. Savage – you look as if you are going to a wedding!" "I am – mine!" I panted. There was no time to stop and I have no idea why he should have been at Waterloo at that time of the morning – but I knew that it was a good omen!

The wedding was quiet and made quieter by the heat. We all sat wilting on the lawn and Valerie's elderly cousin Reginald, a senior civil servant in boots, could not be persuaded to remove his waistcoat. Afterwards, we returned to London to the Euston Hotel, ready to leave with the company for Glasgow in the morning. We were armed with a packet of left-overs from the party; the journey would be long even without the inevitable delays and food was not always available. It was hotter than ever, if possible, next day. After a lunch of whalemeat steak (a great treat) the restaurant service collapsed, there was nothing to drink at all and the wedding left-overs turned out to be very salty anchovy canapés. It was late at night when we finally checked in at the Grand Hotel, Charing Cross in Glasgow, our tongues literally hanging out.

The hotel had recently been vacated by the Americans and seemed bright and fresh with new paint but I managed to contract salmonella poisoning three days later from a trifle made with dried egg – if mixed with water and left to stand for any length of time dried egg was very dangerous. Bath and loo *en suite* were things of the future and I was forced to take refuge in the "Ladies" which was opposite our room

118

and reply only in embarrassed squeaks to Valerie's anxious enquiries. The doctor was called but luckily the attack was short-lived, the weather continued to be magnificent, even Sauciehall Street looked cheerful and Ben Lomond was fully visible for the first time in years – or so a local inhabitant assured me.

Rankl had insisted on taking the entire orchestra on the tour, just to be on the safe side, so there were far too many of us and people were so bored they were begging to be allowed to play. We started rehearsals at once for "Tristan" and for "Rigoletto" which was produced in Glasgow. Stage bands were always "cued in", i.e. played by the orchestra in the pit, on tour and I went to play the E flat clarinet and witnessed a very curious phenomenon on the first night of "Rigoletto". The Duke, tenor Kenneth Neate (an Australian ex-policeman) was sitting at a table for the opening of Act II and pushed back his chair as he rose for his recitative bewailing the loss of Gilda. The chair scraping on the stage gave out a distinct note which Neate took as the first note he sang – but it wasn't the right one. The leader, Jo Shadwick, had to keep playing the correct note loudly and repeatedly to get him back into the right key.

It was on this tour that Constance Shacklock sang her first "Carmen". She was always a very whole-hearted performer, given in her early days to impromptu asides like: "Well, you know what he's like!" which were audible in the front stalls. As she was making her escape while being led off to jail at the end of the first act she knocked over not only the guard but a portion of the scenery as well. In a later performance she would attack Don José, (Edgar Evans) so vehemently with the knife in Act III that he was slightly wounded. Still, it was all in the cause of *verismo*.

When we left Glasgow after two weeks for Liverpool and Manchester I had to put Valerie on the train home, having taken care to book seats for her for at least three of the performances of the Vienna State Opera at Covent Garden to help pass the time until she could join me again in Birmingham. There we could stay with Aunt Dollie, now a widow. She was still saying: "You can't get it now" about every item of food we mentioned and also had a terrible and I hope unique habit of warming up the leathery breakfast toast for supper – but I was very fond of her. I had had my first experience of chamber music with her and Uncle Ernest long before the war. They had a regular quartet, retiring to their rooms to practise for the whole

119

day beforehand, and I had been allowed to play the Mozart and Brahms clarinet quintets with them. They had been very surprised to find how competent I had become in two or three years, I remember; and it is always particularly satisfying to impress elderly relatives.

In Manchester something dreadful happened. We were using the Hallé Orchestra's rehearsal room on the top floor of an old warehouse and were trooping down several flights of stairs while the porters hired for the tour were clearing up. Among our fiddle players at that time was a very pretty young Canadian with clouds of long dark hair, Jean Gilbert. There was a sudden crash and an appalling scream – a xylophone carelessly handled on the top floor had fallen over the balustrade and struck Jean's left hand as it rested on the handrail. She never played the violin again although, after operations and physiotherapy, she was once more able to play the piano which had always been her second instrument and became the solo pianist for the Ballet until she married and went to live in the States. I believe her fight for compensation was a very lengthy one.

And so, after eight weeks, we returned to London at the beginning of October 1947. All our future tours would be in the spring and sometimes only for six weeks which was more than enough with no touring allowance and, later, a magnificent £3 a week. I had good connections with various low-priced commercial hotels from my LPO war-time tours but even they soon wanted £7 or £8 a week. Some of the orchestra were quite happy in real old-style theatrical digs and in the interests of economy I once let Reg Crick, one of the second fiddles and a real old pro from the Carl Rosa days, book me in at Ma Harris's in Acker Street, Manchester. Never again. Ma Harris was quite square and never seemed to take her grimy apron off or her grimy thumb out of the mounds of food on greasy plates which she served us after the show and which I could never face. She would summon us to this terrifying meal with loud cries of: "Come on youse buggers, supper's ready!" Even with our shoestring family finances, I had to draw the line!

· 23 ·

IN spite of the "Opera in English" policy, "Tristan" was always sung in German, even in 1947. "Die Walküre", given on its own in the 47–48 season, was in English and Flagstad and Hotter wrestled valiantly with the text but after that the "Ring" was always in German. When Maria Callas came to sing "Norma" and "Il Trovatore" in 1952–3 she sang in Italian – and so, very gradually, the whole concept both of Opera in English and of a repertory company giving a large number of performances of each opera at various times throughout the season was whittled away. By the advent of Georg Solti in 1961 we had reverted to the old *stagione* system, a series of half a dozen performances only of each very carefully prepared work. These were usually with international stars and always in the original language – even in Russian which meant phonetic translations hand-written into all the vocal material. The only exception I can recall was Schoenberg's "Moses and Aaron" which was for some reason given in English.

Our first production of a Russian opera, "Boris Godunov" in 1948 was interesting as it was finally decided that we should present the original Mussorgsky version, not the one orchestrated by Rimsky-Korsakov which was then more widely known and is still used in the Soviet Union. It is now fashionable to sneer at Rimsky-Korsakov's orchestration as lessening the impact of the work and being too lush and "Hollywood". We certainly no longer need his corrections of Mussorgsky's so-called harmonic "mistakes" which were simply too harsh for the time when the opera was written. Nevertheless, Rimsky made a workable, practical, theatrical version – notably in the Coronation Scene which Mussorgsky's original is disastrously short and without any build-up to a satisfactory climax. The range of voice demanded by Mussorgsky for the part of Boris is incredible and some

121

alterations had to be made to accommodate the singer. Somehow the "Star" got hold of this and carried a little paragraph: ". . . Tonight's version will have three bars of music that are neither Mussorgsky nor Rimsky Korsakov. To avoid an awkward change of key in one of the Boris songs they have been inserted by Temple Savage, Covent Garden librarian, who looks after scores and edits them for use."

"Boris Godunov" was produced by Peter Brook who wrought the chorus to such a pitch that on the first night they behaved like true revolutionaries and beat the chorister playing the part of the peasant Kruschev black and blue. If it had been a film this could have been captured permanently but in repertory the tension gradually lessens and audiences later in the season may well have wondered what all the fuss was about.

The idea of calling on famous producers from the world of straight theatre was an innovation and a far cry from the pre-war days when Charlie Moor, the stage manager, did it all. It was not without problems at first until the special operatic criteria were fully appreciated. Tyrone Guthrie came first to produce "La Traviata" and immediately directed the chorus ladies to dance prettily across the stage in the first scene, hand in hand and crinolines swaying – but with their backs to the conductor! Once matters were explained to him he soon adapted although his original idea for the stage band in the same scene seemed to me distinctly odd. All the guests at Violetta's party swept off into another room to dance whereupon the orchestra appeared at the back of the stage to play for nobody at all. This was changed eventually but I was one of the unfortunates who had to dress up in hussar's uniform crowned with a tall shako that wobbled perilously as I made my way across the stage to my place. Guthrie had sent a message to Jo Shadwick: "No ladies in the stage band, please" but Jo took no notice. He always had a plentiful supply of orchestra ladies – finding them easier to manage, I suppose – and there were some very tight fits among the hussar uniforms. I never liked playing on stage in costume, especially if I needed to memorize the part as I did for "Der Freischütz" in 1954. I was sweating with terror as well as being dressed like a village idiot in a smock, straw-like wig and three-cornered hat, rather like something out of the "Two Ronnies".

Little matters like players who needed spectacles to see the part were never taken into account and in the first "Aida" we all had half-masks, glasses had somehow to be accommodated over or under these and

122

were generally steamed up with agitation anyway – I was thankful I did not then need to wear them. For "Don Giovanni" in 1962 we had kneebreeches, stockings and pumps made in our own size but someone else must have been wearing mine one night and I had to impersonate an old lame player as I hobbled on in shoes two sizes too small. The final insult was that whereas pre-war we had earned a good 13/6d for each stage band (and I never had to dress up) now we were offered exactly 2/6d which was increased to 5/- if we had to put on a beastly costume.

Two stage designs from the very first season have stayed in my mind. The first was Tanya Moisewitch's beautiful, evocative sea-shore with breakwaters and nets for "Peter Grimes" but it gave rise to a very incongruous situation. The people of Aldeburgh, instead of flitting across from the Moot Hall to Auntie's pub with the church in the background, as indicated in the stage directions, danced madly on the pebbly beach in the middle of the night. The band was there too and Auntie had brought out the beer to sell from a little table – all most unlikely on the Suffolk coast in winter.

Salvador Dali's designs for "Salome" in 1949 were quite astounding. There was a curious central pavilion, surmounted with a cluster of what appeared to be wire coat hangers. The whole night sky was the spread tail of a vast peacock; this was splendid although the effect of the whole design was one of icy chill rather than torrid decadence. Dali did want to have a flying hippopotamus as well and Peter Brook had to dissuade him. The costumes were not only very surreal but very uncomfortable; the Salome, Ljuba Welitsch, flatly refused to wear Dali's design and poor Constance Shacklock as Herodias looked like a walking Punch and Judy show, peering out from a yellow tent on a rigid frame. Edgar Evans as Narraboth had an orange Belisha beacon on a long wire sprouting from his helmet and such sharp curved projections on his armour at hip level that he was afraid to fall down when he was killed. Rankl disliked the sets so intensely he played the piano at rehearsals and made Peter Gellhorn conduct; and yet, watching the rehearsal from the back of the stalls, I heard the soft jingle of coins in pocket that always heralded the approach of the General Administrator:

"There, Savage, that's the true Oscar Wilde" he said with satisfaction.

"Yes, but we're doing Strauss's opera" I muttered crossly.

Magnificent singers joined the company during the first years: Elisabeth Schwarzkopf, Irmgard Seefried, the baritone Paolo Silveri, the tenor Rudolf Schock; and the orchestra, playing together regularly and with adequate rehearsals was acquiring a corporate identity – the brass section at that time was particularly fine. All that was needed was someone to bring us to life but until the return of Erich Kleiber in 1950 we were giving routine performances, no disasters but no ecstasy. Rankl, Gellhorn and Goodall were joined by Warwick Braithwaite – I remember that he suggested it was too much to combine the jobs of bass clarinet and librarian and he had a friend who would do the latter job very well. Luckily nothing came of it.

Individual performances stand out in my mind for odd and diverse reasons. On May 19th 1948 my eldest daughter, Imogen, was born while I was playing the prelude to "Rosenkavalier". The maternity home got their wires crossed and for some hours I thought that I had a son; I was not in the least disappointed when I found out the truth. In an early "Tristan" I had a terrible experience but the trouble was that whenever I told anyone about it they burst out laughing. I got hiccups during the second act where there is an extended solo passage for the bass clarinet, known in the profession as "the Death Leap", during King Mark's scene. It must have been sheer willpower that enabled me to space out the spasms to coincide with the places where I took a breath – and the phrases are all very long indeed. To do Rankl justice, he was very sympathetic when I first told him and it was not until he went home to tell his wife who went into fits of laughter that he began to see the funny side. I don't think I ever became quite detached enough for that.

The vagaries of principal singers have engraved two other performances on my memory. For "Il Trovatore" the very high tenor aria in Act III – "Di quella pira" – was often shortened to one verse and also transposed down a tone or semi-tone, so often that we only had the lower version in the Goodwin and Tabb parts we were using at the time. Walter Midgley wanted to sing it at the original pitch and include the second verse. There was not much time and I ended up brewing black coffee and sitting up most of the night working on it. Next day the Press Officer, Michael Wood asked me why I looked so bleary-eyed; when I told him he thought it worth giving to the Press and the "Star" paragraph began: "The fact that Walter Midgley has a fine, strong voice and knows it has occasioned a great deal of hard work for

Mr. Temple Savage . . . amending the score. He has had to write out 150 pages of manuscript." Walter Midgley was very upset, he said it made him appear very inconsiderate, keeping me up all night – I think he even threatened not to sing at all, which would hardly have helped. He need not have worried, it was all in the day's work for me; but when I made new parts I took care to ensure that all three possible versions were included.

Muriel Brunskill, the contralto, was the other artist who wanted an alteration. She asked for her last outburst as Ortrud in "Lohengrin" in 1949 to be put down a minor third.

"But that's ridiculous!" I complained to Rankl. "It will be off the bottom of some of the instruments."

"Put it down a semi-tone, she won't notice," he said. So I did, and she didn't – or at least she never complained.

This same year, 1949, saw the first performance of Sir Arthur Bliss's opera, "The Olympians". It is worthy of mention in that it was the first new English work to be produced at Covent Garden after the war. Otherwise, in spite of a good first act and a libretto by J. B. Priestley, it was largely unmemorable and never revived. Someone who would have good reason to remember it would be Michael Langdon, the bass and internationally-acclaimed Baron Ochs, who was first promoted from the chorus to a small part at short notice while on tour in Edinburgh. Rankl always objected to his choristers taking small parts and so Langdon left to become a soloist.

· 24 ·

IN the summer of 1949 we left our furnished flat in Kensington where it was becoming increasingly difficult to pay the rent and moved into the ground-floor flat of my mother-in-law's large stockbroker-Tudor house in Woking. She had shared it since 1947 with a lifelong friend but once they lived together the two ladies no longer got on so well. My mother-in-law never really cared much for anyone but her own family and had been suggesting that we might come down for some time. For three pounds a week we had a very spacious flat, three-quarters of an acre of garden for the children to play in, (two more little girls arrived in 1950 and 1952, Josephine and Alison) and above all a built-in granny-baby-sitter. An orchestra wife has to face a life of lonely evenings and I was thankful to know that mine would always have company and support, as well as being able to come to first nights more or less whenever she wanted.

My mother-in-law, Mimi, was a very tiny but very forceful person, full of commonsense and very generous towards us. She was also the soul of discretion and would apologize if she came into our sitting-room and found me there – which wasn't often as I was out all day and several evenings a week. At other times, it is true, she dominated the household and even took to blowing a whistle in her later years to summon daughter or granddaughters to the foot of the stairs to take instructions which she would call over the bannisters. We understood each other; she would say to Valerie: "I know if I ask Richard to do something and he doesn't reply, he doesn't mean to do it." I was, however, generally co-operative and we lived in harmony for twenty-three years which may well be a record.

The train service to Woking was, and still is excellent. I could even catch the last one at 11.55 after "Götterdämmerung". I bought a bicycle and for five years, until we could afford our first car, I cycled the mile to and from the station wet or fine and quite often in the snow. With my season ticket at just over £3 a month I could come home for a short break if I had to play in the evening as well as work in the library all day.

The library work was naturally increasing all the time; by 1949 I had moved from the bowels of the earth practically to the top of the building and had a fair-sized room with two real windows. I had also acquired several helpers: J. Arthur Kellet, a retired member of the chorus, looked after all the chorus music and Robert Gwynne who had been a pre-war chorister came as general factotum and continued to work with me until well into his eighties. Tim Killar, my very accurate and hard-working copyist, was one of the great eccentrics of the Opera House. Enormously fat, of grimy appearance and chain-smoking endlessly as he worked, he was by nature a walking disaster area. The stories about him were endless – and true. Tim had patted a horse and it had bitten him; he had cadged a lift on a fire engine and they had crashed into a lamp-post; a hornet had stung him in the chest; he had pulled the chain and the cistern had fallen on his head. It is hardly surprising that when he asked Douglas Robinson, the Chorus Master, for a lift the answer was "Not on your life!" The administration would complain to me of his unpunctuality but my answer was always that as he didn't mind how late he worked it really did not matter in the end. He finally reached stardom in 1959 when Franco Zefferelli, looking for a really scruffy extra to play the village priest in "Cavalleria Rusticana", saw Tim rolling past and more or less shouted "Eureka!" He had friends throughout the theatre but his health was bad and not helped by his great bulk; he suffered a massive heart attack and after a long illness died in the early seventies; at his funeral in St. Paul's, Covent Garden the church was packed.

We remained in our dark attic for fourteen years. In 1960 Georg Solti, being taken on a swift tour of the theatre, put his head round the door and said: "My God! It looks like Niebelheim." Sometimes we felt we were forgotten men. It is true that quantities of the memoranda known as "yellow perils" would reach me, bearing strange messages about lighting rehearsals or who would be dancing the Lilac Fairy on Tuesday but virtually nothing official came my way about what operas would be coming into the repertory. This vital information I had for many years to extract by my usual methods of asking around among my friends in the music staff, or even watching for little paragraphs in the Press. The Royal Ballet had to be more co-operative as so much of their music had to be specially arranged and copied for them, then the ballet conductors Robert Irving, Hugo Rignold and, later, John Lanchbery would come up to see me. In fact, so often were "Swan Lake" and "Sleeping Beauty" cut, uncut, augmented and rearranged in different orders that not for any amount of money would I ever consider copying them again!

Sometimes in the early years I would try to make an appointment with David Webster to ask for an increase in salary but he always seemed to be leaving at once for a prolonged visit to the States and I became quite low-spirited until, like a breath of life, not one but two of my five giants, Erich Kleiber and Clemens Krauss, came to conduct in the same season, 1950–51. It was a Saturday morning when Rankl, whose days as Musical Director were then numbered, introduced Kleiber to the orchestra and scurried away. I could not help wondering for a moment whether it would all be as I remembered. Would the magic still work? How would the new players react to him? I could not help thinking of the anti-climax after Beecham's return. I need not have worried; he had the orchestra in the palm of his hand from the first movement. Even a hard-bitten old cellist who used to grind away down at the bottom and didn't care for anyone said to me with shining eyes: "I wouldn't have believed I could enjoy a Saturday morning rehearsal so much! And he finished half an hour early!" After the first night of the revival of "Rosenkavalier" the Press said: "Dr. Kleiber appeared to have brought his own orchestra with him", so instantaneous was the change he had wrought with the hypnotic power of his eyes as much as with his impeccable stick technique. He could be very severe but he always knew how and when to make a joke and had a very infectious laugh. And always he was on our side against the Management!

"What – no row?" he was reputed to ask with a twinkle. "Then I make one!" He was to conduct a new production of Tschaikowsky's "Queen of Spades" and at the first orchestral rehearsal the hall, somewhere in Holborn, was freezing. David Webster was sent for and told that under no circumstances would he allow his orchestra to rehearse without adequate heating, we were all sent out for coffee and radiators were found and switched on. On subsequent days also the Administration had to check that the hall had reached the correct temperature before Kleiber would start his rehearsal.

I had difficulty with the score of "Queen of Spades", the only one I could obtain was a poor lithographed specimen and not at all clear. When I explained that I could not get anything better Kleiber said he would ask the Berlin Staatsoper to send him one; at that time they were very keen to have him as their musical director. After some while he summoned me to his room early in the morning before rehearsal and showed me a beautiful score which had just arrived. "But they have sent me 'Eugene Onegin' " he said resignedly.

After the first night Kleiber sent for me again. "This must be cutted" he said. "Last night I get a feeling in the back of my neck, the audience are bored – we must cut." I asked him if they made cuts in the USSR as he had conducted there but he said the Russians were quite happy to sit there all night. When we revived it years later with a Russian conductor, Alexander Melik-Pashayev, we did open all the cuts and it was incredibly tedious, there is no doubt Kleiber was right.

Kleiber was not only imperturbable in a crisis, he also actively enjoyed it. One night while I was playing for the "Queen of Spades" Edgar Evans, the tenor in the role of Hermann, staggered forward, pistol in hand, to shoot himself. I could just see him from my place in the pit and expected to hear the usual shot fired by the stage manager off-stage. Nothing happened and Edgar disappeared from my view but I could see the maestro was enjoying himself hugely. I discovered later that, after making repeated useless gestures with the pistol, Edgar Evans had decided with great presence of mind that there was nothing to be done but to seize a dagger from one of the other card-playing officers in the scene and stab himself to death.

So many of these operatic mishaps have passed from one story-teller to another that I have on occasion been told coldly, when relating one of my own personal experiences, that this event took place somewhere else and in another opera. I can only say that I have no need of "set pieces"; if I tell a story then I *was there*! A particular example of this "Russian Scandal" effect concerns a night on tour in Manchester in the fifties (most disasters seemed to happen on tour) when, the pit being too small to seat the full orchestra for "Aïda", we had to open the door under the stage and overflow into the passage. As the Radames called pathetically in the last scene in the tomb: "Aïda, where art thou?" he was answered by a rusty clanking and flushing from the stage hands' lavatory which could be clearly heard in the auditorium and was greeted by a roar of laughter. Now it appears that

David Franklin has told this story in "Great Operatic Disasters" as having happened with Glydebourne in Edinburgh during "Don Giovanni" – it may have, all I know is that it did happen in "Aïda" and I was there!

I was once again on duty in the stage band when Kleiber conducted "Rigoletto". The first thing he did was to reseat the orchestra with the brass in the centre which he said was in the "Italian style". He was an absolute purist about everything that was sung: any attempt by Walter Midgley to soar up to an extra top note would be greeted with: "Is there a B flat there? Have you your score?" When we toured later on Midgley said with relief that he would now be able to sing a "de-Kleiberized" version. In fairness to singers, these embellishments and accretions are more or less traditional – in fact Puccini would write *oppure* with an alternative high note in the appropriate places. I cannot feel that with Verdi's experience of Italian artists he would have minded or been at all surprised at a few trimmings. Certainly, though, Kleiber's stimulating influence could be felt in the performance, especially in the great Vengeance duet at the end of Act II between Rigoletto and Gilda which he insisted must pass through no less than seven stages of increasing and carefully controlled intensity. The effect was electrifying.

I was not normally involved in "Carmen" but Kleiber asked me to be available backstage for the second act when Don José is heard approaching, singing the difficult unaccompanied "Dragoon of Alcalà". He said that he knew from experience that tenors were apt to wander off key a trifle at this point and I was to keep close to Edgar Evans, playing the tune on the clarinet but very softly and an octave higher: apparently in this way it could not be heard in the front of the house. I do not know of any other conductor who did this, although it must have lessened the strain for the singer considerably.

Nobody had troubled to tell Karl Rankl that Clemens Krauss had also been engaged that season to conduct "Tristan" and "Fidelio": the first he knew of it was when he saw it already printed in one of the throwaway publicity leaflets. It seemed that he was now totally disregarded. Krauss was immensely tall, immensely aristocratic. He was reputed to be the son of a Viennese dancer and a member of the Hapsburg family, he certainly seemed to have the "Hapsburg lip". He dressed in flowing cloak and wide-brimmed hat, spoke perfect English and told me once that his favourite author was Charles Dickens. To the orchestra he was invariably calm and courteous; his baton was very long and his beat very small. We had a minimum of rehearsals for his "Tristan" and were even unable to get right through the piece at the general rehearsal but he was perfectly prepared to sort things out at the performance. He placed his white handkerchief on the desk in front of him and would hold it up quietly in his left hand to warn us of a difficult moment to come. I have never again felt the hairs on the back of my neck tingle as they did in the "Death Motif" in Krauss's "Tristan". He was to return for the 1952–53 season but I only played the last act of "Die Meistersinger" with him as it was the practice in those days (introduced by Rankl) to change the principals of woodwind and horns for this final act which is over two hours long and longer than the other two acts put together.

It was rumoured that he might become our next Musical Director but he left to conduct the opera in Mexico City, although he had a heart condition. The altitude brought on a fatal attack not long afterwards. Whatever plans there may have been originally, there followed an interregnum of three years without any Musical Director being appointed, a very unsatisfactory state of affairs.

· 25 ·

I HAVE not given much space so far in these pages to the Royal Ballet although I had to play for them quite regularly. I confess frankly that, except in my young days when I was eager to play everything to gain experience, I did not generally enjoy playing for ballet as much as for opera unless it was something like one of the Stravinsky ballets, "Firebird", "Petrouchka", "Rite of Spring" or Ravel's "Daphnis and Chloé". Fonteyn might be dancing but, seated under the overhang of the stage, there was nothing to see and nothing to relieve the monotony except the faint pattering of feet; it made it all seem rather a slog. Sometimes new players would welcome it, saying: "Thank God, no bloody singers tonight" but they soon began to miss them and the feeling of being part of a dramatic whole after the experience of an entire evening of strict balletic tempi. The general rule seemed to be that the music must be made to fit the dancers and not the other way round, the only exception in my experience being the Bolshoi company whose interpretations were very musical. I also preferred to play for specially commissioned works as I have an invincible objection to a work created specifically in one medium being made use of as part of another, for example, it seems quite indefensible to me to make a ballet to Mahler's "Kindertotenlieder" or "Das Lied von der Erde" where the combination of voice and orchestra is quite enough for a complete artistic experience without the addition (I would say detraction) of dance. If existing music is used, I think its original form should be observed as closely as possible but even the great choreographer Sir Frederick Ashton was cavalier in his treatment of Mendelssohn's music when he was creating his ballet "The Dream", pulling the Scherzo to bits which he then put back in different places to suit his requirements. In a commissioned work, if composer and choreographer were *en rapport*, pitfalls could be avoided, which is

132

why the Stravinsky ballets are so incomparable and why the Ashton-Lanchbery collaboration in "La Fille Mal Gardée" produced the most enchanting ballet of the last twenty-five years. On the other hand, when John Cranko choreographed Britten's "Prince of the Pagodas" in 1952 the dancers complained that the dances were far too long, there was too much music. The composer resolutely refused to make any cuts, more or less telling them to twirl round a few more times. He simply could not realize that for once the audience would not be there primarily to hear his music.

With the production of Constant Lambert's last ballet "Tiresias" in 1951 and his death not long afterwards it was the end of an era for the Royal Ballet. He had been with them since the early Vic-Wells days before the war. Sadly, he was by now almost incapable of further work. The ballet had been composed a year before but we were anxiously awaiting the orchestration in order to prepare the parts. All he brought us was the first number on outsize manuscript paper that would not fit into any folder, the rest arrived in small sections which had been orchestrated by a number of his friends: Robert Irving, Dennis ApIvor, Christian Darnton, Elizabeth Lutyens and Dr. Gordon Jacob.

Lambert had decided to use an orchestra without violins or violas, with a large wind section, cellos, basses, percussion and solo piano. As the first performance drew near I was away on tour and Tim Killar was copying day and night. At the final rehearsal Lambert decided that he needed a few more bars as an Interlude and this he dictated in the stalls to the hapless Tim who was obliged to lie on the floor as the only flat surface on which to write. He then copied the parts, passing them over to the players in the pit as he finished each one.

The ballet was over an hour long and was not received with rapture, the number portraying the copulation of two snakes giving a certain amount of offence to an audience in 1951. By being drastically cut it was shortened to fifty minutes and in the following years I took the opportunity of editing out some of the discrepancies in orchestration arising from its having been scored by a committee! I had to make a new full score anyway as every orchestrator seemed to have used a different size of paper and it was impossible to bind it all together in a presentable fashion.

As Librarian my involvement with the creation of a new ballet could be more considerable than this. In 1952 Ashton wanted to present

133

Delibes' "Sylvia". There was no full score published, only a piano version which they conducted from in Paris. We had the orchestral parts sent over and I had to make a full score from them. Fortunately we had ample time as the first thing I discovered was that there were no orchestral parts for several numbers in the first two acts. In reply to our enquiries the French publishers said that as these numbers were never performed at the Opéra they did not trouble to print them. So I had to orchestrate them myself, not too difficult a task after copying out so much Delibes. But there was still more to do; Ashton wanted to embellish the third act with various extra divertissements. This music was taken from another Delibes ballet "La Source" and orchestrated chiefly by Robert Irving, the ballet's new Musical Director, with one number by myself. This full score I had made was then the only one of "Sylvia" in existence. As for "Coppélia", the only full score we had was of the third act which had been orchestrated by Dr. Gordon Jacob in 1946. The French never performed more than the first two acts and seemed incapable of imagining that anyone else might want to do what they did not. I decided some time later to make a full score of Acts I and II of "Coppelia" and that also, as far as I know was the only one in existence although the French did ultimately publish Delibes' own orchestration of Act III.

While the Royal Ballet were on tour we would be visited by various companies from Europe and the States. I would slip in to watch rehearsals and particularly enjoyed the joyful, vigorous, athletic dancing of the Americans in works like "Fancy Free", "Rodeo", "Billy the Kid" and "Age of Anxiety". I have good reason to remember that one of the New York City company's ballets was to Stravinsky's "Orfeo" as that was the night on which an elderly and demented bassoon player decided to hide the clarinet parts in the prompt box where they were not discovered until the following day. He was violently infatuated with Olive Wright, our first clarinet, who was not down to play that evening and in his poor muddled mind this represented a slight upon his beloved's capabilities, so he felt that if she could not play no one else should. This did not come to light until later, all Bernard Bree and I knew when we went into the pit was that we had no music for the second ballet. Frantic messages to the orchestral porters produced no spares so I ran out in the interval to see if by any chance there was a second full score. There was, I doubled back with it and with my finger firmly on the right line to guide him Bernard

134

managed to play the first clarinet part. Every so often I added a few notes of the second clarinet when I felt it safe to remove my finger from the page for a moment. We were lucky to have Robert Irving as guest conductor that evening, he both sympathized with our plight and appreciated our valiant efforts to fulfil our obligations. As can be imagined, the bassoonist left shortly afterwards; he had been a very fine player but he was creating an impossible situation by insisting that he was the only member of the orchestra playing in tune when the truth was quite the reverse.

The Americans did not care a fig for our copyright laws which last until fifty years after a composer's death. I was horrified to discover that one company was about to open that very night with a ballet to a completely rearranged "Variations on a Nursery Theme" by Dohnanyi who had only died in the thirties. I hastened up to the General Administrator's office and the managing director of the American company was immediately summoned and told that either the music must be played as the composer had written it or the ballet would have to be cancelled. There really was no time to alter anything and in the end David Webster's diplomacy produced a compromise – the publishers would allow one single performance of the ballet on payment of a heavy indemnity and an undertaking never to perform it again in this country.

The De Cuevas company from Monte Carlo were not very strong on matters of communication. One of their programmes consisted of a ballet to Mozart's "Eine Kleine Nachtmusik" – "Concerto Barocco", requiring only strings, followed by "Noir et Blanc" to music by Lalo which needed a large orchestra. One matinee they suddenly decided to reverse the order of the programme without notifying the players. The conductor arrived in the pit to find only strings as usual and the scurrying to and fro as the staff of the orchestra office tried to round up the others from the neighbouring pubs was something to behold.

The repertory of the Paris Opera Ballet was full of sonorous classical titles like "Phèdre", "Nauteos" and "Icare". This last ballet had been created for Serge Lifar, one of Diaghelev's company, now old and rather past it but still dancing. Scored for percussion only it needed so many players that the orchestral manager himself was on the cymbals, but the conductor kept complaining irritably about the poor quality of the cymbal playing and we soon noticed the manager had replaced himself!

135

1951, FESTIVAL of Britain Year, saw the first performance of Vaughan Williams' "Pilgrim's Progress". It was conducted by Leonard Hancock, one of the music staff, a fair, good-looking young man, so quiet and relaxed that Beecham asked in a loud aside after meeting him for the first time: "Does he breathe?" Vaughan Williams had announced rudely and publicly that he did not want "any of the Opera House hacks" to conduct his work but it didn't really matter who conducted it; as Kleiber said when I asked him his opinion of it: "Nothing much you can do with it, is there?" It just went on and on in a pleasant, undramatic way.

Beecham was also to return to the Opera House for the first time since the war. I can see him coming into the pit for the first orchestral rehearsal of "Die Meistersinger", looking up at the great crimson curtains, visibly moved and murmuring: "Very pretty." Then he plunged straight into the Prelude and the theatre was filled with the special golden sound that he could conjure from an orchestra. After that happy moment the rows began, just as in the old days, while Lady Betty sat in the stalls and made notes about various players.

"Some of these players must go" says Sir Thomas to Morris Smith, the orchestral manager. "I have a list here of players I can call upon." Unfortunately they had all recently been fired by us! He did not get his way but he never stopped trying.

I was not needed for "Meistersinger" as Beecham would not allow relief players to take over for the last act but at 4 p.m., when the first performance was due to start at 6, my phone rang and to my amazement it was Sir Thomas. He could not find the chorus master, he informed me, and wished to call all the extra chorus for rehearsal half an hour before the show. I was a name from the old days so he expected me to find the solution. I managed to get him transferred to

Cliff Clifford, the stage director who, I'm afraid, gave him short shrift as the extra chorus were not called until 9 p.m. and could not possibly be expected to return before then. I still had to go to see Beecham in person.

"Mr. Savage, I have some marks I want put in for tonight." He showed me his score.

"That's all right, Sir Thomas, I've already done it."

"What do you mean? How could you know?"

"It's what you always like – a crescendo at the end of Act I." One up to me. I could catch my usual train to Woking.

Beecham had also been given the choice of a new production in the summer and everyone hoped for something like Delius's "A Village Romeo and Juliet" but he decided on Balfe's "Bohemian Girl" – source of that famous Victorian drawing-room number "I dreamed I dwelt in marble halls" which, incidentally, was most beautifully sung in this production by a young American, Roberta Peters. He did not even select the original version but one made subsequently for Paris with all sorts of interpolations. It was produced in Liverpool at the end of a tour in which Rankl had conducted Flagstad's farewell performance in "Tristan". I believe the birth-pangs at production and piano rehearsals with the singers were fearful. I was thankful only to be concerned with the orchestral ones and that was enough. We ran a sweepstake as to how long the general rehearsal would go on for, it started at about four and finished round about eleven-thirty at night. I had an extended obbligato on the basset-horn for the aria "When other lips and other hearts" and there was even a placed marked "cadenza".

"What do I do about this cadenza, Sir Thomas?"

"Go away and write yourself one."

So I hurriedly consulted Norman del Mar, who conducted most of the performances as Beecham soon seemed to lose interest, and between us we concocted something in time.

During the rehearsals Tim Killar, already up to his eyes in work on Lambert's "Tiresias", had to come up to Liverpool and stay at the Adelphi, sharing a room with Beecham's personal librarian, Brownfoot, in order to be on hand for all the little alterations and insertions the maestro was constantly making. I did manage to slip home for one weekend with my family when it was "Swan Lake" on the Saturday and I was not needed, but only on condition that poor

Tim stayed in case "Tommy" should have any new ideas on the Sunday.

There were two casts, in the first the tenor was an American, Anthony Marlowe, known I'm afraid as Larry the Lamb on account of his very quick vibrato, but in the second cast it was that inimitable Australian artist, John Lanigan, making the first appearance of what was to be a career of over thirty years at Covent Garden, progressing through all the romantic roles to a series of perfect, unforgettable character portraits. Amongst so many perhaps his Shuisky in "Boris Godunov", his Rector in "Peter Grimes" and the wonderful vignette of the Inkeeper in "Bevenuto Cellini" spring at once to my mind.

When we returned to London we gave "Bohemian Girl" every night for a further two weeks and it was broadcast. Before the days of tape recorders a number of firms would make acetate records to order from broadcasts. Roberta Peters commissioned the whole opera and I ordered the third act from the same firm to include my famous basset-horn obbligato. My usual ill-luck in such matters prevailed and it transpired that the BBC recording engineers had not switched on again after the interval until "When other lips" was over and my glorious moment was lost to posterity.

The interregnum period was certainly not devoid of highlights. In December of 1951 came the first performance of Britten's naval opera "Billy Budd". It was originally supposed to have been conducted by Josef Krips of the Vienna State Opera but he withdrew at the last moment, saying that his poor eyesight (he wore thick pebble lenses) made it too difficult for him to learn the score. This seemed odd to me as Britten's manuscript was perfectly clear. Perhaps he did not care for the work although it is one of the composer's greatest. One can only speculate; anyway, Ben himself came to conduct and he certainly knew his job. He also had the ability, unusual in a composer, to explain to us clearly in words what he required from us in music.

The preliminary rehearsal had been taken by Peter Gellhorn who had received instructions from Britten that his metronome markings must be strictly observed. Peter prepared us with his usual meticulous care but when Ben finally arrived to conduct his actual tempi bore little relation to those he had originally insisted upon! We had an identical experience in 1963 when Shostakovitch arrived to listen to rehearsals of his "Katerina Ismailova" conducted by Edward Downes, also in accordance with the composer's own metronome markings in the score.

The original sets by John Piper were so realistic that the moment the curtain went up one was transported aboard the "Indomitable" where the crew were holystoning the deck. The more impressionistic sets in a later production gave me none of that intensely claustrophobic feeling of being on a real ship at sea. An undeniable success in England in spite of its lack of love interest and all-male cast, it seemed an odd choice for us to take to Paris for a few days the following spring. Ben used to duck nervously during the ensemble where the officers sing: "Don't like the French, don't like their hoppity-skippety ways – those damned Mounseers" and we noticed that by the last act the audience had thinned noticeably. Still, I could enjoy the four days, it was May, Valerie had been able to come with me and we had time to visit friends made on a recent Brittany holiday. We had one of those vast French meals with them, it lasted three hours, the plates were changed innumerable times and the wines changed with them while the jokes grew bluer and bluer. I was soon lost but Valerie said afterwards she wished she had been less fluent in French as she couldn't pretend not to understand them.

"Billy Budd" was followed in January 1952 by the first stage production in this country of Berg's "Wozzeck", conducted by Kleiber. Before rehearsals started every player had been given an English libretto to read, to help us understand the work more thoroughly. This was his normal practice for all new works when he was Musical Director at the Berlin Staatsoper. We had nineteen rehearsals in all with separate sectional ones for strings, brass and woodwind. He took infinite pains with us; Berg's notation does not make it easy for the players at times but with Kleiber everything became crystal-clear, as usual. At the final rehearsal he told us that he was pleased, we were not to worry. "Just think you are playing a Haydn symphony." He cancelled the second of the two general rehearsals, confident that it was not necessary and might even be harmful.

There were fourteen scene changes, sometimes with barely enough music to cover them. In the third act the scene change takes place during two terrifying crescendi on one note (B natural) which should last for a total of fifteen seconds. During this time all the furniture for a tavern scene, including a special out-of-tune piano, had to be put in position. Kleiber said he would hold the note for a maximum of twenty seconds, then he would have to go on. On the first night, sitting under the stage, I could hear all hell break loose over my head. Fifteen, sixteen, seventeen . . . then, with three seconds to go, suddenly all was quiet. It would only have needed the piano lid falling on a stage hand's fingers to wreck the whole thing.

The second act of "Wozzeck" ends curiously with four silent bars, two of them with pauses marked over them, the last two in tempo as the curtain falls. Kleiber used to beat these solemnly and told us at rehearsal that, in Berlin, one critic had suggested that Dr. Kleiber did not know the score as he was still conducting when everything was over.

He was with us through 1952 and 1953 for more spendid "Rosenkavaliers", "Tristan" and a marvellous new "Elektra" with Edith Coates as a tremendous Clytemnestra, after which we were to see him no more. In the long dull days of touring, Howell Glynne, the Baron Ochs in "Rosenkavalier" at that time, used to love to tell of the night when he appeared to have totally lost his voice. In spite of his whispered protestations that he could not possibly sing, Kleiber, who had come to his dressing-room, told him not to worry: "Just leave it to me." When the Baron's first entry came, Kleiber drew an expressive finger across his throat and gestured to us to play pianissimo. At first Howell really had no voice but he gradually grew in confidence until by the end of the opera he was singing in full voice – no one quite knows how unless, as I genuinely believe, the force of Kleiber's personality was literally hypnotic.

I had a minor mechanical disaster of my own one night in "Rosenkavalier", the first since the hiccups in "Tristan", which not even Kleiber could solve. We had hardly started playing when the pad came off a key on my basset-horn and I missed quite a bit while I felt about on the floor for it, had the good luck to find it and ram it back on the instrument where it held until the end of the performance. After the first act I hurried round to apologize to the maestro. "Don't worry – I sang it for you," he reassured me. "And anyway, only you and I and Strauss in Heaven will have noticed."

Quite simply, there has never been anyone like him.

140

· 27 ·

THOMAS MATTHEWS had come from Manchester to succeed Joseph Shadwick as our leader, bringing with him as deputy Charles Taylor. When Matthews left to go to Singapore Charlie became leader and David Webster expressed the hope that we would have no more changes; he did, in fact, stay with us for over twenty-five years and this was of inestimable help. During the interregnum we were, like the LPO during the war, playing under the batons of a quantity of different conductors, some better than others, some very good indeed but we were losing our individual style again, becoming a "utility" orchestra. In addition to the resident conductors, Barbirolli came frequently, John Pritchard came, Tausky came – as well as Dobrowen, a Russian from Paris, and no less than three Italian conductors; Capuana, Erede and Gui. Gui conducted "Norma" for Maria Callas's first appearance in this country in November 1952. She was then still stout and bespectacled but her voice was never more splendid. I was playing in the stage band, which seemed to go on for most of the opera in spite of Gui's extensive cuts, and could see the floor of the stage for the first act marked out with luminous paint so that the myopic diva could make her way safely up and down the various levels through the sacred wood to cut the mistletoe. At this time Callas made no attempt to use her latent dramatic abilities, she just stood with folded arms, emitting a stream of wonderful sounds. She sang "Casta Diva" in the original key – a tone higher than anyone sings it nowadays, but she said no one seemed to have noticed and so she would not put herself to any more trouble; in subsequent seasons we put it down a tone once more.

Famous for her rages in other opera houses, the "Tigress" was perfectly amenable at Covent Garden, thanks to the skill and tact of David Webster. "Sir David is a gentleman" she always said. Towards

141

young and pretty singers I think she could be less kind. Leonne Mills, a tall, slim, attractive girl with no lack of self-confidence, had the small role of Inez, Leonora's confidante in "Il Trovatore". Callas had apparently been disagreeable to her one evening, "So," she told me gleefully, "I went out before the show and ate a large pickled onion and then I sang my first line: "Ha! dunque . . ." right in her face." Leonne Mills married well, I believe, and left the stage; a pity, one feels, with spirit like that she should have gone far.

1953 was Coronation Year and an opera had been commissioned from Benjamin Britten. I cannot help feeling that they made the wrong choice of composer for the kind of piece they wanted, William Walton had a great sense of occasion and would probably have produced something more suitable. Britten always needed to be inspired by the words of his very literary libretti but Walton would have enjoyed the pomp and circumstance. Be that as it may, what we got was "Gloriana". The opening jousting scene was effective and the Elizabethan pastiches, where the ballet danced to unaccompanied chorus, were charming if not entirely successful; dancers need more vigorous rhythm than unaccompanied voices can provide. The whole idea of presenting a charming young Queen with a portrait of her illustrious predecessor as aged, bald and agonizing over the Earl of Essex seemed to many people to be rather tasteless. Valerie, in the balcony stalls, could catch a glimpse of the Royal Box and was convinced that Prince Philip was reading a green and white Penguin thriller behind his open programme – and who can blame him? At the end of the opera the applause trickled away into silence before Ben had arrived on stage to take his bow. I heard a very distinguished-looking elderly person in the front stalls exclaim loudly: "My God! They've got him in the Tower pretty quick!"

1953 was not only Coronation Year but Centenary Year in what was then still Rhodesia. The whole company was to go to Bulawayo for six weeks in the summer, taking "Aïda", "Bohème", "Figaro" and inevitably, "Gloriana". Everyone was to be vaccinated and I was not at all happy about this, never having been done as a child and suspecting that, at forty-four years old, the consequences might be dire. Could I please stay behind and play second clarinet for the ballet? No – I was needed for three out of the four operas we were taking. So I was vaccinated, developed vaccine fever and had never felt so ill in my life. I had just recovered sufficiently to be taken by taxi to Blackbushe

Airport and put on the plane where the air hostess dosed me regularly with Veganin each time the fever recurred. Only two people managed to stay behind, one second fiddle, who had also never been vaccinated and was not considered to be essential, and Morris Smith the orchestral manager, who was afraid of flying and always seemed to get his own way, for reasons which I suspect were connected with his membership of the Freemasons. Frank Stead was in charge and managed perfectly well; we also took a different stage manager specially for the tour, Pat McClellan, I have never forgotten him as he appeared in full Highland dress at all times.

Jets and pressurization were still a novelty, though Peter Gellhorn was lucky enough to fly out later on a Comet. We were in an old-fashioned Hercules, seated facing the rear of the plane which was supposed to be safer. We touched down at Malta for dinner the first night, Wadi Halfa for breakfast, had coffee at Khartoum and dinner the second night at Entebbe in Uganda. We spent the night there and I saw fireflies for the first time, little winking greenish traffic-lights on the side of the road. The next leg of the flight took us to Livingstone, circling over the Victoria Falls en route. Now we had to change planes as Bulawayo airport could not, at that time, accommodate the larger aircraft. About half a dozen of us were left behind for the whole afternoon as they could not fit us on the first flight; we were the lucky ones as the airport officials organized an outing for us to the Falls, only a short drive away, where we had a happy afternoon, were drenched with spray and found our car covered with baboons. It was pitch dark by the time we boarded our Dakota and we could see bush fires in spreading circles glowing below us.

On arrival we were met by David Webster in his overcoat as it was winter there and after day-time temperatures of 70–80 degrees Fahrenheit darkness and sub-zero temperatures would arrive simultaneously at six o'clock every evening. It was a severe winter and the flowers for the Queen Mother's visit shortly before had all been killed by the frost before her arrival. We were loaded on to a bus and taken about three miles out of Bulawayo to Centenary City, a vast complex of chalets surrounding a central leisure area with restaurant, bars and lounges. Here the rank and file of the company were lodged together with general visitors to the Exhibition. The Centre for this was built just on the outskirts of Bulawayo and included a vast theatre, hollowed out of the side of a small hill to provide a natural rake for the stalls. An underground stream had been discovered in the orchestra pit and the damp was never really eliminated. At first the pit was filled with malodorous paraffin heaters and we all played wearing every available vest and pullover under our evening shirts which made us look strange and misshapen. Although the land seemed flat it was actually a plateau some 3,000 feet above sea level and in consequence the singers found themselves a little short of breath at times although we had a week before the first performance in which to acclimatize ourselves. The railway line ran behind the theatre, only a quarter of a mile away and throughout our stay the shows were interrupted regularly at the most unfortunate moments by the long, loud whistling of the night mail as it approached the level crossing. There seemed at first to be no solution as the drivers refused to stop whistling on the grounds that it would be dangerous. Gradually, by adjusting the length of the interval for each opera, shortening one here, lengthening another there, they managed rather cleverly to avoid the most poignant scenes being ruined by this prolonged banshee wailing.

After recovering from my vaccination I remained fit and well throughout our stay but there was a good deal of the usual stomach trouble attendant on such trips which was decimating the orchestra, especially the trumpets. We had taken six in order to have extras for the fanfares in "Gloriana" and "Aïda" but we rarely mustered a full complement, even for the operas that did not require extras. I think we were all nervous of becoming ill, we had no financial security and we remembered poor Louis Yudkin, the stage director, who had been sent out ahead of the company, died suddenly and had left a wife and young child more or less destitute. There were so many horrible tropical diseases we could catch – in particular, the lake was marked by a skull and crossbones sign and the word "Bilhartzia", warning against bathing because of an appalling intestinal parasite which would stay with you for life. Only Wilfred Smith, the flautist who never took notice of anything official because it could not apply to him, went swimming all the same. When we returned to England he began to feel unwell and although it proved to be nothing serious he panicked, ringing up Morris Smith to cry off rehearsal.

"I can't come in today, I'm ill," he wailed. "I think I've got bilhartzia.'

"Oh, I don't know him," replied the orchestral manager whose mind was always on his work. "Is he a good player?"

We strolled round the Exhibition Centre, saw Gary Cooper in "Mr. Deeds goes to town", already far from new, had an outing to see Rhodes'grave in the Matopo hills, went to lunch with some people to whom I had been given an introduction – and after that I was consumed with boredom. Four roads led out of Bulawayo, north, south, east and west but whichever way you went it was always the same: "Miles and miles of damn all" as the pilot of our Dakota had described it. When the bus bringing us back each day to Cemetery City, as it soon became known, turned off the main road we could see a little petrol station with a sinister sign: "Fill up here, no more petrol for 750 miles." My chalet faced an identical chalet and the rear window looked out on the bush; I envied our principal cellist in the opposite chalet, he sat in the doorway at his easel, painting in water colours. All I could so was write home every day, asking for news of my three-year old daughter who had been taken into Great Ormond Street Hospital for an operation on her neck just before I left England; it was about two weeks before I knew that all was well.

A small measure of excitement was provided by Matthew, the black boy who looked after me. He was incapable of filling the paraffin heater without flooding the floor as well and I was constantly expecting fire to break out. I also had to keep looking under the bed for snakes. One day some of us decided to walk the three miles into Bulawayo although we had finally been given free bus passes, after protesting loudly that we could not afford the daily fares. Nobody could believe we really wanted to walk and every car that passed stopped to offer us a lift. Eventually it became so hot that we had to give in and accept one. And every day I could see the little mail plane coming in to land and all I wanted was to be on it for its return journey.

To make matters worse the beer was terrible and full of gas. Tom Neville, the orchestral porter who, if not quite so gloomy as Wally Knight was just as much of a character, christened it "Coffin Cocoa" and when you offered to buy him a pint was apt to say thank you he'd rather have the one-and-six. It was certainly very cheap and this, combined with the general tedium, had a very deleterious effect on our harpist, James Gibb. He had been loaned to the Hallé Orchestra who had been in Bulawayo before us and as it was not worth while flying him home again he had to await our arrival, spending long hours in the bar and becoming seriously addicted. At the general rehearsal of "Aïda", as off-stage harp in the second act, he simply would not stop playing – every time he got to the end he started off again and finally had to be prised from his instrument by the stage manager.

David Webster had gone home so I was sent for by his deputy, Sir Steuart Wilson, as the Sultan of Zanzibar was due to arrive and his national anthem must be scored in case he decided to visit the opera. This anthem turned out to have been written by the late Sir Donald Francis Tovey and was immensely long.

"We can't possibly do all that," said Sir Steuart, "it's like a Beethoven Sonata. I'll find out how little we can get away with." I scored the truncated version but it was wasted effort as the Sultan decided not to go to the opera. This must have been the first of many similar tasks that fell to my lot over the years and which do not normally come within a librarian's terms of reference. Among others were Greece, Portugal, Lebanon, Syria and especially Guinea in 1959 when the House Manager, John Collins, sent me a memo to tell me the President of Guinea and his party were "thrilled by the playing of their National Anthem and thought the orchestration the best they had ever heard" – adding unofficially that he'd hoped to get me the Order of the Camel second class but had not had any success!

And now at last came the longed-for journey home. After temperatures of 112 degrees in Khartoum so that the sweat literally burst out of us as soon as we stepped out of the plane, we were touching down at Blackbushe again. There were a few clouds in the summer sky, there was green grass instead of thorn trees and singing birds instead of the great black African crows – and my two little girls jumping up and down beyond the Customs barrier. We were home.

· 28 ·

ON our return from Rhodesia we had a brief holiday while the Bavarian State Opera from Munich performed three Strauss works at Covent Garden, "Arabella" and his last two operas "Die Liebe der Dane" and "Capriccio". Their Musical Director was my fourth giant, Rudolf Kempe who was quite unknown in England at that time. He made such an enormous impression with his command and understanding of Strauss's music that David Webster immediately signed him up for the revival of "Salome" in our forthcoming 1953–54 season.

Kempe was tall and very quiet with strange slanting dark eyes; when he first came to us he had hardly any English at all but he could count and manage the rehearsal numbers. His only other phrase was: "The same", which served to indicate to us that he wanted to repeat a passage. He had no real need of words, he conveyed everything with his expression and his hands; and his stick technique was of unsurpassed clarity. "Salome" starts with a very soft rising scale on the clarinet and we were accustomed to a certain amount of anticipatory flailing from Rankl. At the first rehearsal Kempe gave a small, neat flick with his baton and Olive Wright, the first clarinet, was bewildered and did not come in. Kempe was firm; he made it plain that this was all that was really needed and we soon became used to the small beat which was in fact perfectly clear. The results were atonishing; like Kleiber, Kempe produced such an effect on the whole orchestra that we would have followed him to a man through fire and flood. He had been a fine oboe player himself, with the Leipzig Gewandhaus Orchestra, and this increased his affinity with the players while his skill and experience as a piano accompanist made him the ideal conductor where singers were concerned.

He was to come to us regularly over the next ten years, conducting a wide variety of works and setting a standard to which we could keep even when he was not with us. After "Salome" came a superb "Elektra" and then "Rosenkavalier". Although the latter did not have quite the ultimate champagne sparkle of Kleiber's, the delicacy and beauty of sound he obtained were absolute, helping the singers to ride the storms and enabling the words to be heard at all times, something he considered to be of vital importance. "Without the words it is so boring" he was able to explain to us as his English improved.

Later on he would conduct practically all the Wagner operas but not immediately as the first "Ring" cycle after the departure of Rankl had already been allotted to Dr. Fritz Stiedry. He was quite an elderly gentleman who had been first Kapellmeister at the Berlin State Opera in the twenties and had long expected to become Musical Director. Instead, Kleiber, years his junior, was appointed over his head and there ensued a good deal of in-fighting. Eventually Stiedry left and went to conduct in Russia. He obviously knew the "Ring" thoroughly but he did not go down well with the orchestra. He was extremely opinionated and made it clear that he did not think much of us, closing any discussion with: "There can be no question but I am right and you are wrong," which was not calculated to endear him to us. The performances, as I remember them, went well but they made no impression on me. Next season, 1954–55, when Kempe took over, it was a very different matter. Once again his insistence on hearing the words meant that everything orchestral was toned down but not simply kept down, on the contrary, it was all graduated and scaled in the most masterly way so that after two or three cycles of his "Ring" I came to feel, as we opened with the first scene of "Rheingold", that everything was already prepared for what was to ensue four nights later at the end of "Götterdämmerung". His entire "Ring" was marvellously constructed as a whole and not just as four separate operas.

Once or twice players, particularly the brass, complained that he wanted them to play so softly it was not humanly possible. His argument was that he sought to create at Covent Garden, with its open pit, the same effect as at Bayreuth. There, with the orchestra below the stage, a good strong tone would not swamp the singers but we must inevitably make adjustments. In the end he succeeded, as always, but it was very hard for the brass to deliver what he wanted from them.

He was convinced, and he convinced us, that if you play exactly as the composer has indicated you cannot go wrong and yet, in spite of his exact observation of Puccini's markings in "Madame Butterfly", he managed to avoid the usual feeling of constant stops and starts which arises from the rather awkwardly written short phrases. He kept the music seamless and flowing, creating the only wholly satisfactory performances of this opera that I have ever heard. He had two highly-acclaimed Butterflies, Amy Shuard and Victoria de los Angeles but for some unknown reason was not *en rapport* with the enchanting Spanish singer; he never said anything but always appeared unhappy during her performances; obviously not caring for her interpretation.

His "Tannhaüser" in 1955 was the first production of the opera since the war with rather unfortunate sets by Ralph Koltai. One critic described the landscape in which Tannhäuser finds himself on leaving the Venusberg as resembling one of the drearier stretches of the A3. There were certainly a great many frail, blackened trees on a brownish heath, such as we often see in my own part of Surrey after a summer fire on the common. No consideration seemed to have been given to the vocal problems of the singers – the Hall of Song in Act II was so vast and open that it was utterly lacking in resonance and Silvia Fisher as Elisabeth had difficulty in projecting her voice over the orchestra, all the sound seemed to go up into the flies. Kempe was very upset by all this and I can see him walking up and down in the stalls, his head in his hands, asking the world at large if something could not be done. Nothing was.

This was a good example of the prevalent trend towards very diversified preparation by designers, producers and musical directors instead of their being at one in their view of how the work in question should be presented. Before the war, in the great ensembles like Berlin, Munich and Vienna, a unified conception would be thrashed out as it were in committee between the various departments. Now our designers were preparing sets and costumes without consultation with the Musical Director and so we had the "Tannhäuser" situation of a set in which singers could not sing. Another case in point is Puccini's "Turandot" in which the stage brass band (of six trumpets and four trombones) plays a considerable role throughout the opera. Puccini specifies that in the great Riddle scene and the final apotheosis the band should be placed centre stage behind a gauze only, so that they can blow straight out into the auditorium to crown the climaxes. I

149

remember this well from pre-war performances. The composer's instructions were not strictly adhered to in our 1947 production as the band was behind solid scenery, not a gauze, but it still made some impact. Cecil Beaton's very pretty fairytale sets for the 1963 production, on the other hand, made no provision at all for the stage band which finally had to be lodged in the stage boxes, entirely visible and blowing across the audience instead of out at them, much to the annoyance of Edward Downes, the conductor, who could not obtain the effect he wanted.

When Kleiber had taken over our production of "Figaro" in the 1951–52 season he had been horrified to discover that the set for the last act bore no resemblance to the scene prescribed in the text where the various characters must be seen to be paired off in different little pavilions; there was just a general garden scene which made nonsense of the multiple situations and misunderstandings. Kleiber did actually succeed in having the whole set redesigned and I remember arguing fiercely about it with Ande Anderson (later to become Stage Director) who considered that the Musical Director had no right to meddle with the stage production. Only Kleiber was determined enough to get his way – other conductors had to take what was put before them. There were, of course, exceptions; the two great Italian designers Luigi Visconti and Franco Zefferelli. Visconti made a careful allowance of space for the stage band in the "auto da fé" scene in "Don Carlos" and both men expected to collaborate closely with their musical directors.

· 29 ·

A GREAT deal seems to have happened in the 1954–55 season. As well as Kempe's first "Ring" there were premières, only a few weeks part, of two new works by British composers: William Walton's "Troilus and Cressida" on December 3rd 1954 and Michael Tippett's first opera, "A Midsummer Marriage" on January 27th 1955. We also knew by now that we were to have a Musical Director again, Rafael Kubelik, who came to give his "test piece", Smetana's "The Bartered Bride" in May 1955. And the General Administrator had a new Assistant – John Tooley. This last event was of personal significance for me. After eight years I was still clamouring plaintively and intermittently for a salary increase; now, suddenly, a fair, handsome young man appeared in the Library, examined everything that was being done, talked to me in a friendly fashion – and soon afterwards I got my rise. It was good to know that from now on there was someone in authority who was accessible, interested and who cared.

Walton was a slow worker and his opera had been simmering for some time; he was often dissatisfied with what he had written and when I saw him at a first night and asked how it was going he answered, with his usual quiet twinkle: "Not too well, it keeps sounding like "Cav and Pag!" It didn't, of course, and proved to be good romantic stuff. It was entrusted to Sir Malcolm Sargent who had conducted the first performance of "Belshazzar's Feast" and other Walton works.

Sargent had not changed since the pre-war days when he had tried his hand at Charpentier's "Louise". He still did not seem well acquainted with the score, he was still an inveterate fiddler and tamperer with other people's works and he still did not relate well to the singers. He always addressed them by the name of their role in the opera: "Troilus" for Richard Lewis and "Pandarus" for Peter Pears

151

and so on. It must have made them feel like mere ciphers and certainly gave offence. Perhaps he never knew their real names! Like the pre-war Italian conductors, he refused to beat unless the orchestra was playing but, whereas in Italian opera it is often a matter of pure recitative, here Sir Malcolm was leaving whole ensembles to fend for themselves without setting them a tempo; he would let them start and then join in with the orchestra. Peter Pears came forward at rehearsal and begged him to give them a beat but he still refused, saying he would feel such a fool, conducting without the orchestra. The murmured acid comments from the pit can be left to the imagination.

As for the alterations, they were legion. Every afternoon after the rehearsal all the material (which was full of inaccuracies anyway as it had not been properly checked by the publishers, later we had to make a fresh set,) had to be carried up four flights to the Library where Walton would join me with the score to look through all Sargent's recommendations and make alterations which we then had to transfer to all the parts. Sargent had a particular aversion to anything written for two harps and was constantly cutting out bits of the second harp part. One day Walton came upstairs looking particularly disgruntled and suddenly burst out: "I'm not making any more alterations. It's my fucking opera and I'm going to write some *more* for the second harp!" which he proceeded to do and this seemed to have the desired effect, I do not remember many more alterations.

Walton knew how to write for the various instruments, it was always grateful to play, however difficult. If there were problems he was always ready to listen to the player's point of view and make adjustments. Michael Tippett did not seem to have quite the same professional understanding of the technique of various instruments. I was not in the orchestra for "A Midsummer Marriage" and only played for one Tippett opera, "King Priam" in 1962 when I recall that the composer could not be persuaded by Charles Taylor, the leader, to agree to the alteration of one single note in a very rapid passage for the violins; it was a technical point, would have made the passage playable and would have been unnoticeable at that speed. At the first few performances John Pritchard transferred the passage, whenever it occurred, to the piano part where it did not present a problem but in the revival the composer persuaded Brian Balkwill to restore it to the strings with what I thought to be rather unfortunate results. I do not feel that I should pontificate at length about Tippett's music which has

152

never spoken to me as other composers have. There is no doubt that he created some ravishing sounds in 'Midsummer Marriage", and the "Ritual Dances" in particular are now well-known in concert performance, but the ideas in his libretto were abstruse and not immediately accessible, especially as the words lay uneasily on his vocal line. There always seemed to me to be too many notes, producing a thick and clotted effect; my lack of appreciation must remain my loss.

Rafael Kubelik's "Bartered Bride" in May 1955 was a thoroughly gay and sparking affair with its authentic Czech rhythms and I always think of the word "aristocratic" in connection with his performances. I did a considerable amount of work for him: I made the full score of his "Libera Me" for publication by Universal Edition and the piano reduction of his short opera, "The Emperor's New Clothes" (though someone else had to put in the Czech words) and I copied for him the works of this father, Jan Kubelik, the violinist. I found him to be a charming man and liked him very much. He was perhaps a little too amiable to be the Director of a great opera house and would sometimes appear to over-compensate for his indecision by a burst of harshness; on the whole he was well described by someone who referred to him as "the velvet hand in the velvet glove". His first production as Musical Director was a very fine "Otello" in October 1955 with Ramon Vinay and Gré Brouwenstijn and sets by Wakhevitch. Unfortunately it lacked that great artist, Tito Gobbi, as Iago and we were all shocked to hear that he had been replaced at the last minute. Gobbi recounts in his autobiography, "My Life", how he arrived late on a foggy evening and, phoning from the airport, found that only the final act was being rehearsed at that moment. As Iago only has a few phrases in that act he decided to get some rest and reported to the theatre the following morning only to find that Kubelik, who always made something of a fetish of rehearsals, had already replaced him by Otakar Kraus. Gobbi was deeply wounded and this unhappy incident shows how Kubelik could over-react. It also, in the end, showed the generosity of spirit of both men. Kubelik apologized publicly and handsomely at a party at David Webster's the following summer and Gobbi accepted the apology without continuing bitterness.

Kubelik was a very fine musician and obtained fine performances although I could not say that his influence on the orchestra was comparable to that of Kleiber or Kempe. He was something of a fuss-pot at rehearsal and this was reflected in his beat. He needed to talk a great deal to get what he wanted and this never goes down well with British orchestras. He was, however, unfailingly kind and during his three years in office he insisted that there should be no changes in the orchestral personnel unless someone wanted to leave for a good reason. Before that there had been far too much coming and going as the management suddenly decided not to renew contracts at the end of a season. Now we could settle down for a while and become an ensemble.

After "Otello" came a new "Magic Flute" which I found rather precious and for which we had no less than fourteen rehearsals. We were nearly driven mad; as Kempe said, when he took over (after one rehearsal): "What can you do with the "Flute" except play it?" The 1956–57 season was more exciting with Janáček's "Jenufa" and Berlioz' "The Trojans" both for the first time at Covent Garden. The cast for "Jenufa" was superb, including Amy Shuard and John Lanigan, and with Czech music Kubelik was once more in his element.

"The Trojans" is in two parts – the Fall of Troy and the Trojans at Carthage. In Paris often the first part was performed on its own and never previously had the work been given in its entirety in one evening. It was performed virtually without cuts except for some of the dance music and a portion of the last act. I also remember having to condense the two stage bands into one and they then had to play up in the paint frame, backstage. We still had no closed-circuit television, only a loud-speaker so that John Matheson who was conducting the stage band, knew when to come in. On the first night the loud speaker broke down just before their entry and all John Matheson could do was count and hope it would work out all right – which it did. The press had become very enthusiastic about the Dido, an American called Blanche Thebom. In the final immolation scene, the public were told, her long hair would be worn loose and would reach well below her waist. It proved to be rather a disappointment; it was long, certainly, but did not look very luxuriant and the chorus ladies went about telling people that it was full of additional false switches. She was not a particularly memorable singer; the touching song of the young sailor, Hylas, longing for his homeland, sung by Dermot Troy who died tragically young, is perhaps what lingered longest in my mind. There was also the most moving mime by a young dancer, Wishmary Hunt,

154

as the widowed Andromache silently mourning the loss of Hector, to the accompaniment of a very long clarinet solo. Gielgud was producing and at first would have liked to cut the scene as it presented such a problem for him but it was pointed out that this was one of the musical highlights of the opera. I believe he would have liked Dame Peggy Ashcroft to do it but the slender, fragile grace of a dancer was exactly what was needed to realize the pathos of the scene.

"The Trojans" was revived twice, under John Pritchard and Colin Davis, but I still think of those first Kubelik performances as the best, he had a great affinity with Berlioz' music. With Wagner it was another matter. For "Die Meistersinger", a lyrical and cheerful work, things went quite well but his "Tristan" in 1958 was an unhappy event from the first orchestral rehearsal – he did not seem to understand the idiom, nothing was shaped in the way to which we had become accustomed and as a result everything fell apart. It was booed on the first night and I would rather not dwell on it.

Francis Poulenc's "Dialogues des Carmélites" in the same year was a far cry from the subject matter of his early opera, "Les Mamelles de Tirésias". Strongly anti-clerical myself, I could not stomach all the French religiosity but the work had been revived several times and is still very popular with students, probably on account of the numerous female roles. The bass clarinet part was awkward and some of it lay so high that Kubelik considered putting it down an octave. The composer had come over to England and I was able to ask him if he really wanted it so high and he said yes so I was obliged to tell the maestro that I would have to play it as written whether I liked it or not.

1958 was to be the last year for Kubelik, his contract was not renewed and we had another short interregnum before the advent of Georg Solti in 1960 but now Kempe was still coming to us regularly so our standards were not allowed to fall. My fifth and final giant, Carlo-Maria Giulini, had first appeared in May 1958 to conduct Verdi's "Don Carlos" in the most splendidly elegant production by Luigi Visconti with Tito Gobbi as Rodrigo and Boris Christoff as Philip II. Giulini, like Kempe, had very little English at first, he would attract our attention by saying gently: "My gentlemen . . " I felt at once that this was how Verdi should be played, with a wonderful springing rhythm and singing quality – "sempre cantare" he would say and even in the staccató passages would give the apparently contradictory instruction: "Staccato – ma sempre legato" which somehow we understand quite easily! After he had visited the States his English unfortunately became much more fluent and he was inclined to talk at length, which he had no need to do. Although I saw comparatively little of him in the pit at the Opera House, I did also play for him with the Philharmonia in the Mozart Requiem. Always very serious, his face, as well as his hands, was most expressive, he appeared to be undergoing an almost mystical experience as he conducted and his approach never seemed to me to be typically Italian, it was less extrovert and especially sensitive. Perhaps that is why his "Barber of Seville" in 1960 did not seem so satisfying – the humour of this opera is too broad and obvious.

So now I have no more giants left. In the outside world wars and invasions may be reported, presidents be assassinated, revolution break out but the world of opera is a crystallized one. We might perhaps get a trendy production of "Die Walküre" with the Valkyries on motorbikes, or even a topless "Carmen" but the music of Wagner and Bizet is the same for ever and the seasons come round with "Rings" in the autumn and spring tours, as steadily as the natural seasons. I run the risk of becoming a Parson Woodford of the Opera House: "boiled beef and dumplings today" while the mob guillotine the king and queen of France – only with the name of an opera substituted for the menu. But this is a risk I have to take. I can only tell it as it really was.

· 30 ·

IN 1957 my father, in spite of a lifetime of healthy vegetarian living, collapsed and died, aged seventy-nine, on Raynes Park Station while unwisely running for a train. Ironically, his elder brothers outlived him and I think an inadequately-nursed bronchitis not long before must have strained his heart. He had astounded us all five years previously by marrying again – a redhead called Winnie but who had to be known as Veronica in accordance with his usual practice of rebaptizing his lady friends. She was in her thirties, only a few years older than my own wife, and seemed sensible so we were much relieved and hoped she would take care of him. Within a few years of his death she married yet another elderly gentleman so it must have been quite a way of life for her. In all fairness, her reasons for taking on my father can hardly have been mercenary as he was constantly in fearful financial straits. He was a strange and gifted man; as an adult I found it difficult to share in his manifold enthusiasms but when I was a child he was a wise and encouraging parent and it is probably from him that I inherited my somewhat rebellious individuality and also a certain amount of philosophic detachment which stood me in good stead during the endless rail journeys of the war years and made me a patient commuter ever afterwards.

It was fortunate that I was such a good traveller as I would often make the journey between Woking and Waterloo four times a day. It was essential to have that short break in the afternoon if I had to play in the evening as well as work in the Library; and I was so near Waterloo that the quickest and cheapest solution was to go home for a couple of hours and have a poached egg on toast, travelling on my season ticket. My family suggested that what I needed was some kind of club in London and for a short while I joined "Mainly Musicians", an elegant establishment which had opened near Park Lane. It had a good restaurant but nothing more than a cup of tea was available before a show and there was nowhere in the handsome formal reception rooms where I could stretch out for the indispensable snooze. It was also awkward to get to and from the theatre so I went on travelling home. I would fall asleep the minute I boarded the train and wake up as we passed Sorbo works, a few hundred yards outside Woking. Only once in twenty-three years did I oversleep and was carried on to Basingstoke. It was on a free evening and I caught the next train back, arriving home just in time for a dinner-party – luckily, as I had all the drink with me.

Calm and philosophic I may have been but it was a wearing life and I was now nearly fifty while my three daughters were no longer jolly babies but strong-minded little females of seven, nine and eleven. I got to bed late, they had to be up early for school and the house was filled with the clashes of their extrovert personalities. Finally, something snapped and I behaved quite out of character.

In 1959 Callas was to perform in Cherubini's "Medée" and she had arrived with her tame conductor, Antonio Rescigno, who insisted on having the orchestral parts that had been used when Madame had sung it in Texas. Ricordi's had sent us two sets of parts as they were not sure which was the correct one. Rescigno made his choice and my staff and I were obliged to stay until nearly ten at night, working with Rescigno to put in all the various dynamics. He was a pleasant little man, he had two little girls, I had three and we chatted and worked happily. In addition, I had already had to call at the Waldorf Hotel that morning to collect chorus parts of the "Messiah" as Beecham had persuaded David Webster (soon to become Sir David) that he needed "reliable help" in marking them all. In the train home I tried to start on this new task but the thought of the mounds of monotonous work that lay ahead, after a very long day, wrought me to such a pitch that I could not sleep – an extraordinary occurrence for me. In the morning the little girls were obstreperous at the breakfast table and the cornflakes were flying about. I hurtled out of the front door, aiming a ferocious swipe at my eldest which knocked her against the hatstand and was pursued by her indignant shouts of: "It wasn't me – it was Fina!" Twitching with strain, I arrived at the theatre and as I went in the stage door there was little Rescigno about to go into the pit.

"The parts are all wrong!" he squealed as soon as he saw me.

"What do you mean – wrong?" I roared. "We worked on them with you all yesterday evening!" And I took him round the throat and shook him severely before he broke loose and scurried off in terror. Tom Neville, the porter, put out the other, unmarked set and I never did discover what he had meant. I think Callas must have been bullying him; he was terrified of her.

I went upstairs and sent a message to the Administration to say we could not possibly help Sir Thomas out, we had not the time. Then after a while I began to wonder whether I would be charged with criminal assault, so I went down to the canteen for a cup of coffee to steady my nerves. There I met David Webster's secretary, the imposing Miss Kerr who, to my astonishment, smiled and murmured discreetly: "I hear you nearly strangled Rescigno – a pity you didn't do the job properly." As Geissmar had said long ago when I had answered Sir Thomas back: "Richard, you bloody fool – that *is* the way to do it!" But once every ten years is enough.

To return to more auspicious events, in November of the previous year, 1958, the wind players of the Opera House orchestra had given a concert before Her Majesty the Queen as part of the Leeds Festival. The only work we performed was the great B flat Serenade for thirteen Wind Instruments by Mozart. It was conducted by Benjamin Britten who was not best pleased when we arrived at the University for our first rehearsal to find that no one had thought to provide us with any music stands. We propped the parts up on chairs until Lord Harewood arrived with taxi loads of stands from the Town Hall.

Britten was a very exacting rehearser and he also had his own very individual interpretation of Mozart from the point of view of shaping and phrasing which was surprising in that it was unlike anything I had previously experienced, but entirely satisfying none the less. He obviously had a great love of Mozart's works. During rehearsals, always mindful of problems relating to the National Anthem, I asked whether we were to play it and if so Britten would need to score it for the thirteen wind and give me time to copy the parts before the Saturday concert (it was then about Thursday) as obviously on such an occasion and with such an unusual group of instruments we could hardly "busk" it in good old pre-war fashion. Lord Harewood said he would try to ask Her Majesty about it after dinner that night but next day confessed that the meal had started so late and gone on for so long he had never got round to doing anything about it, so the idea was abandoned. The Serenade lasts a full fifty minutes and must have been something of an ordeal both for the Queen and the Duke of Edinburgh but they were most gracious afterwards when, fortified by Lord Harewood with a glass of sherry each against possible nerves, we were all presented. I was playing the basset-horn and remember the Duke of Edinburgh asking me kindly if it was the only instrument I played, a thought which startled me into replying: "My God, no! If it were I'd starve!"

At the same time the Opera Company were giving Handel's "Samson" in Leeds as well under the baton of Raymond Leppard, and Joan Sutherland caused a sensation with her brilliant rendering of a single aria at the end: "Let the bright seraphim", although it was the following year 1959, which was to be the season of Sutherland's greatest triumph as "Lucia di Lammermoor". I was not involved and so was able to relax and take Valerie to the first night, in some trepidation as we simply could not envisage big, kind, jolly Joan as the doomed and pathetic Lucia. Zefferelli really worked a miracle on that first night, it was touching, convincing and beautiful. Sutherland was transformed, like Trilby under the power of a more benevolent Svengali and long afterwards one would see shreds of what he had taught her clinging to her in other rôles. She was only truly allowed to be herself in Saqui's send-up of "La Fille du Régiment" in 1966. The critics were appalled, they had seen a first night audience rolling about helpless with laughter and that was worse than having fun in church. Instead of the traditional dainty soubrette there was Joan as a huge *vivandiére*, glorying in her size, singing superbly and waltzing about with a minuscule chorister for her partner. The soldiers of the defeated army arrived clad only in their long underwear, cries of "Merde!" were heard as rifles were dropped on toes and it was all most reprehensible – but such a wonderful relief!

Returning to 1960, we also had a little mild fun during the "Ring" when, Kempe being unavailable that year, we played under the baton of a big, cheerful man from Leipzig, Konwitschny. He was perfectly normal at rehearsal but always required a bottle of hock in the intervals at performance. By the end of the evening it was always empty and this made him excessively jolly and he would keep turning round with a beaming smile, apparently to conduct the audience, until Sir David said he was thinking of issuing them with song-sheets for community singing.

The great Otto Klemperer, who came in 1961 and 62 for "Fidelio",

"Magic Flute" and "Lohengrin", was a very serious conductor and not given to levity. He was by now an old man and had become a legend in his lifetime. His heyday had been at the Krolltheater in Berlin even before the Third Reich, when he had conducted all the new works, now he was principal conductor of the Philharmonia. Well over six feet tall, he was always supported into and out of the pit by Clem Ralph, the librarian of the Philharmonia, as he had suffered a severe stroke and serious burns when he had set fire to his bed with his pipe and tried to quench the flames with alcohol instead of water. His performances were always majestic, ponderous and rather loud – he was probably rather deaf as well. Usually the dialogue in the "Magic Flute" is well cut but he not only restored all the bits normally omitted but added more of his own – and then he would nod off during the long stretches of dialogue and have to be woken up for the next aria by the leader. However, he showed such incredible fortitude that the British sporting spirit would have seen that he was cheered to the echo whatever he did.

Meanwhile, in the ballet world the most perennially enchanting of Ashton's works, "La Fille Mal Gardée" was being seen for the first time in 1960. All through the previous year John Lanchbery had been working, while on tour with the second company, to arrange and orchestrate Hérold's early nineteenth century ballet for Sir Fred and the completed sections had been arriving every so often through the post for me to make the orchestral parts. As well as Hérold, Donizetti and Rossini the ballet contained quite an amount of original Lanchbery – notably the now celebrated Clog Dance – and was none the worse for that. Hérold's original orchestration, written in great haste, was not particularly exciting and this was a case when the rescoring really made an improvement. The critics are on the whole very down on this sort of thing and William Mann of "The Times" said to me he would have liked to hear what Hérold originally wrote. I doubt if he would have enjoyed it but this is probably why, when Ashton needed new music for the end of "The Two Pigeons" and Lanchbery wrote a clever blending of previous themes from the ballet to make an effective finale, the fact was not mentioned publicly.

Ever suspicious, William Mann was soon hot on the trail. Since 1947 I had been much given to writing to the papers in defence of Opera House productions and I had come to know him quite well – he once called me his "Opera House Conscience". So he invited me out to

161

lunch and brought a little gentle pressure to bear. I ate up all the lunch but only admitted that it was "some music that had been discovered" (mumbling with my mouth full) – "in an old piano score". I don't suppose he believed me but nothing could be proved. If the critics had known, I wonder if they would have damned the last act?

We used to see a good deal of Jack Lanchbery when my children were young, he would take them to the cinema and to cream teas and he was a wonderful organizer of parlour games. The whole family rose up in protest once during a session of "Categories" when he insisted that "Chocolate-covered ants" counted as an item of food beginning with C. "I'll send you some for Christmas" he promised and a little parcel arrived from Fortnum's. It contained a small tin and a message: "Sorry no chocolate-covered ants left, here are some bumble bees in honey." I was the only member of the family who dared to taste them. We also have somewhere on tape the recording of a chipmunk singing "La Donna è Mobile" which he made with us when we bought our very first tape recorder. His relaxed good humour was also appreciated by the orchestra who used to enjoy rehearsing with "Jolly Jack" as he was affectionately known and I think we generally expected he would become the next Musical Director of the Royal Ballet when Robert Irving left. This was not to be; "Madam" Ninette de Valois would not appoint another Musical Director although Jack was doing everything without being given the actual title. I am sure this must have wounded him deeply and may well have been why we eventually lost him to Australia.

· 31 ·

ALTHOUGH I always hated leaving my family, the prospect of a short Middle East tour to Lebanon, Syria and Greece in August 1961 sounded quite tempting even though it meant playing second clarinet for the ballet. The first clarinet was Fred Lowe who had just joined us and who was to succeed me as bass clarinet before long. Most of the orchestra were in Edinburgh playing "Iphigénie en Tauride" with Solti so our leader was Marie Wilson, formerly sub-leader of the BBC Symphony for many years, while our conductor was Dudley Simpson, then quite unknown as a composer. Dame Margot Fonteyn was starring and red roses were flown out nightly from England for her from her husband. This time we were flying by jet and it was John Tooley who greeted us at Beirut airport where we were parcelled up into fours and fives and put into large taxis. Our driver immediately switched the radio and his headlights on full and tore off with us into the mountains.

It was the most terrifying journey of my life. The road to Zahlé, where we were to stay, seemed to be all hairpin bends and precipices while the headlights kept showing up the unpleasant crushed remains of cars that had also tried to pass this way but had not quite made it. As we rounded one bend we saw not one but two pairs of headlights hurtling towards us and one of the girls in the back gave a little scream and fainted. Our driver plunged between the two cars without turning a hair; driving apart, he was a most amiable man, as were all the Lebanese I met. We passed a magnificent hotel and nightclub in the mountains where Dame Margot and other VIPs would be staying but we were to be lodged at the Hotel Kadri in Zahlé, a town which our driver proudly pointed out as having a river running through it. It was a very smelly one, as were all the middle Eastern rivers I came across but our hotel was comfortable and not particularly oriental.

163

From Zahlé we had to be transported nightly in more terrible taxis along the Bekaa valley to the great complex of temples at Baalbek, built by the Emperor Augustus. The ballet were to perform in the open air on a huge stone platform in the forecourt of the temple of Bacchus where an orchestra pit had been dug out and loudspeakers fixed high up on the lofty stone pillars. From here a Debussy fanfare, known as *le signal*, was broadcast just before the performance started, to summon the audience. The sun would be setting and the sky a deep peacock blue with the spark of a satellite moving rapidly across at the same time each evening.

In the interval, mint tea was served, which I frankly did not care for. Queuing for it near Frederick Ashton that first evening I murmured: "It doesn't seem quite the thing to be drinking in the temple of Bacchus." He agreed with me and at the party on our last night when there was champagne we stole away together and solemnly poured a libation of the real stuff on the altar of the god, to make amends.

After the performance we had to make our own way to the big, unlighted car park to find our taxis and minibuses; it was easy to wander off course in the dark and one night a horn player unexpectedly fell into the nearby river. I had to sit next to him all the way back and the stench was appalling. The road from Baalbek to Zahlé ran straight along the valley and mile after mile of red tail lights were strung out all the way like a chain of rubies as the audience returned home. Our taxi drivers would simply keep their hand on the klaxon and their foot on the accelerator and overtake everyone at breakneck speed, knowing that there was never anything coming the other way at that time of night.

The following week we went on to Syria for two days, travelling by bus past many a crusader's castle to the green oasis of Damascus and arriving to find that there was about to be a revolution. We were advised not to wander in the streets on our own and we had no desire to do so. There were a great many lorries driving about, out of which people kept jumping, diving into cinemas and cafes to drag out struggling victims. I did try to find the tomb of Saladin in the great mosque but took the wrong turning and found instead a bayonet presented at my stomach so I abandoned all ideas of independence and joined the organized tour of the *souk*, the Street called Straight and the house from which St. Paul was reputed to have been let down in a basket, (it didn't look nearly ancient enough to me.)

164

Syria had recently joined the United Arab Republic and there were statues of Nasser everywhere. To avoid National Anthem trouble I had bought a new book of "National Anthems of the World", published only a few months previously, and had been busy orchestrating the ones we would need. In the Lebanon all had gone smoothly but as we started to rehearse the anthem listed as that of the United Arab Republic the liaison officer for Damascus rushed forward in great agitation; on no account must we play that one any more. What and where was the new one, then? He took me off to the old part of the town and there, in a tiny music shop about nine feet square and full of radios, they produced a sheet of music with the required melody. Dudley Simpson made it quite clear that there was no way in which this could be scored for orchestra and the parts copied by that evening. John Field, the company director, thought it would be better to play nothing at all but the resourceful liaison officer then managed to find some parts used by the police band at the local radio station. Although these were for a military band they might possibly be used if enough string players were willing to transpose from them on to their own instruments.

An hour before the performance the orchestra were gathered and as there seemed to be a general atmosphere of indecision I stood up, waving the music sheets and called out to the strings: "Who can transpose from a B flat clarinet part?" I am sorry to say the first violins all declined but the seconds and violas said they would have a go at the second clarinet part and the second oboe was willing to transpose up a minor third to play the E flat clarinet part; the cellos and basses were all right as the brass parts for the military band were written at pitch – and so it went on like some strange parlour game until after a brief run through to see if it worked the local man expressed himself satisfied and an international incident was averted! I should have liked to make a copy of the anthem but it was not allowed.

The usual intestinal alarums and excursions had already begun in Lebanon, the poor girl who had fainted in the back of our taxi on the drive to Zahlé had become so ill after rashly sampling a fly-blown melon on sale by the roadside that she had been taken into hospital. Curiously, I began to feel better in Damascus and it was not until we were in Athens that I was really defeated. On arrival we had a couple of days off and before my stomach finally rebelled I had been with friends on an unforgettable outing – in a hired and clapped-out old

Vauxhall with a slipping clutch, all along the new coast road to the temple of Poseidon at Sunion with the wonderful smell of thyme all round us on the headland. I have always been a lover of things Hellenic and the only false note that day was struck by Marie Wilson who as a devout Catholic felt obliged to disapprove of so much enthusiasm over a pagan site. I did manage the Parthenon and the Museum as well but after that I just had to stay in bed all day and crawl out to play in the evenings, in the Herodes Atticus theatre which has the most wonderful acoustics imaginable. I was feeling too low to take much notice of anything but – yes, there was nearly yet another National Anthem problem; we were rehearsing it, a rather martial piece, when a Greek stage hand called out: "If you play it as slowly as that there will be a revolution!" and Dudley Simpson had to whip up the tempo until the stage hand was satisifed.

After the last performance we were all invited to a party in the lovely gardens of the British Embassy where some local delicacy, whose name I have forgotten but which looked like a vast sausage three feet long and a foot wide, was suspended over a smoky fire. Surrounded by his minions, all in white tuxedos, H. E. himself was carving it for his guests and I must have been feeling a little more stable as I ventured to try a piece and found it delicious. However, I still arrived home next day so many pounds slimmer that I was greeted with cries of horror and sent straight to the doctor for a course of antibiotics. In spite of all this my memories of that tour are happy ones and not least because it was then that I first had the opportunity of getting to know the oboist and cor anglais player, Anthony McColl who was generally to be seen sitting quietly apart, deep in the novels of Henry James but who was to become one of my most valued friends from that day to this.

166

· 32 ·

IDEALLY the ballet "Les Sylphides" should be danced to piano accompaniment, Chopin being notoriously difficult to orchestrate, but the Royal Ballet used the version by Roy Douglas which was as good as any. I cannot imagine why but, at some point in the early sixties – "Sylphides" was performed too often for me to pinpoint a date – Sir Malcolm Sargent was commissioned to make a new orchestration. I can only imagine it was after a heavy lunch date with Sir David. I duly collected the material from Albert Mansions, being very much given to understand that this would be the definitive version of "Sylphides", and prepared a beautiful score and parts. Sir Malcolm was full of praise, even presenting me with a pair of large and quite unwearable mauve cufflinks. The first performances were conducted by Lanchbery but the Press were not invited until Sir Malcolm took over himself. Then William Mann of the "Times" fell upon him, castigating him not only for the generally poor taste of his orchestration but for breaking a basic rule of scoring piano music. He had failed to remember the effect of the sustaining pedal in producing a continuous bass on the piano; as a result there were long passages with the wrong inversion of a chord which gave the wrong bass. This is something every college student of composition would be expected to know; he obviously scored purely from the notes without considering how it would sound. Very much upset by the bad press, Sargent went to complain to Sir David Webster and I heard from Miss Kerr that he had tried to imply that it was all my fault for copying it incorrectly! I then felt quite free to send the awful mauve cuff-links to the jumble and that was my last brush with Sir Malcolm.

Ironically, I was induced to feel some sympathy for Sargent and his rough handling by the Press when I myself, in the late sixties, had to orchestrate Schubert's "Fantasia in F minor for Piano Duet" which

167

was used by David Drew for his ballet "Intrusions". The piano version, successfully used on tour, was felt to be inadequate for the Opera House and a score was to be commissioned. Various orchestrations were submitted and mine was chosen, chiefly because I had taken pains to ensure that it still sounded like Schubert while another more brilliant entry sounded like Rachmaninoff! For this I was to receive the first thoroughly disagreeable notice of my life from John Percival in "The Times" who damned the score as "pedestrian" and myself as the "perpetrator". How easy it is for a critic to slaughter his victim with just two words! I am glad to record that John Tooley phoned me up to assure me that the Management did not agree with the verdict.

George Solti had become our Musical Director in 1960 and was to continue so for ten years. In him we had at last a Director of stature who found great favour with both Press and public, but he came at a bad time for me. I was already of an age and length of experience which inclines one to what Philip Hope-Wallace has called "the kind of regretful sighing criticism . . . ending in the words 'but you should have heard So-and-So'!"* Also I was becoming unhappy with my own playing, it seemed to me that I was no longer always in tune but in the midst of the orchestra could not always hear if I were sharp or flat. I did not intend going as far as that fine trumpet player, Jack Cousins, who retired immediately and permanently after cracking one note but nor did I wish to hang on indefinitely until someone had to tell me that I was past it. It can easily be imagined that my state of mind was not receptive to the sheer relentless drive of Solti's performances. There was certainly an abundance of superficial excitement but in his "Ring" I missed all the things I had valued most in my giants – the shaping of a whole, the insistence on the composer's own dynamics and – although this may come strangely from an instrumentalist – the care taken to ensure that the singers could ride the orchestral sound without strain and the words be clearly audible. There is no doubt that at first there were singers who were upset and disconcerted but now, watching him on television in my retirement as he conducts, or charms an interviewer with his delightful fractured English, I find it quite hard to equate him with that frenetic figure of the early days, urging us on relentlessly with voice, gesture and grimace until John Lanigan

*Philip Hope-Wallace "Words and Music".

christened him "The Screaming Skull". John, of course, was a singer who could remain imperturbable at all times. "John, dear, I beat it in twelve here" Solti called to him at a rehearsal of "L'Heure Espagnole" (where Lanigan played the cuckolded old husband, Torquemada) "Don't worry, Maestro, I never look" came the laconic Australian reply. And I am glad to record that Solti laughed; where I was concerned he just glared – and I glared back.

To add to my trials while playing for Solti I was having tooth trouble; my dentist was still treating an abscess when John Tooley took me at long last to look at a possible new location for the Library in a building facing Long Acre which in my doped state I accepted without demur. Next day as the pain eased I realized that the place was quite unsuitable, being much too far from the actual theatre and I had to ask John Tooley to find somewhere else. This was on the ground floor of 45, Floral Street, exactly opposite the Stage Door and had previously been occupied by a potato merchant. Perhaps this accounted for the strange and enormous beetles in the cellar where we stored all the negatives and tracings; these so horrified my new young assistant, Jane Gore, that she nearly left at once and the Pests Officer was sent for in haste. But now we had glass-fronted cupboards, yards of smooth formica surfaces the length of the large room and a grimy little doorless den off the main library where I could lurk unseen but know all that went on. At last we had, too, our own Library Loo which we immediately locked and defended against all comers, it was the first one available on entering the building and consequently much in demand.

It was Jane who had the excellent idea that all vocal scores should be kept and issued separately from the orchestral material and she vanished with them into the adjoining building, high above the Box Office where they remain to this day. When she left to start her own bookbinding business, Diana Odling left the chorus and took on the job. The only drawback was perhaps, that it meant that one member of the Library staff had to be something of a lone wolf and tended to miss out on the real coffee (instant was forbidden) and ten minutes with the "Times" crossword which became a tradition in the office.

Round about the time of the move to the new quarters I was about to book my digs as usual for the Edinburgh Festival when I discovered that I was not down to play at all the concerts, Fred Lowe was doing several of them but nothing had been mentioned to me. I wrote to John

Tooley at once asking: "Am I still the bass clarinet of this orchestra or not?" and he replied that as far as he was concerned I was – but of course he had to consult Morris Smith. Now I had known Morris since about 1930 and have even shared digs with him for a time and knew him in all his aspects: first as a very bad trombone player – "Who is that terrible trombone, Mr. Smith?" Rankl had asked innocently when Morris himself had been playing in the "Aïda" stage band, heavily masked and unrecognizable; then as a man with an unerring nose for a good player for his orchestra and above all as thoroughly devious, although it was very hard to catch him out. There was nothing to be done, he seemed to be in an invincible position, getting his own way in everything with the catchphrase: "Webster says". Only his Masonic connections can really explain it.

Not surprisingly, there was no love lost between us and he had done his best to drop me in it on many occasions over the years, I knew too much about him. I remember one particularly ludicrous set-to when I received an astonishing memorandum from him to the effect that: "It has been reported to me that you were seen turning to look at the stage during a performance of Die Walküre" (We were at the time on tour in Birmingham where there was no pit and so the orchestra were more visible than usual.) Apparently Lord Harewood thought it looked untidy, something I never really believed. It ranks with Fürtwangler trying to stop us crossing our legs. Anyway, I replied that his memo had been received and the contents noted, only to get another one saying he was waiting for an explanation. So I gave it him – several pages of it and quoting Kleiber's dictum that he could not stand players looking bored when they were not playing, better to leave the pit . . . or show interest in the performance? I could always win an argument but now I was not willing to play the part of the wounded ageing buffalo to be hunted down by Morris Smith. I went to the General Administrator and told him that we were enormously busy in the Library and I thought it better that I should no longer continue to be a regular member of the orchestra as well. The break was by no means total yet, for another few seasons I would still be playing every so often, for operas like "Elektra" or "Die Frau ohne Schatten" where both bass clarinet and basset horn were needed. I was happy that it should be Fred Lowe who succeeded me and gave him my bass clarinet which he continued to use for some time.

The part about being so busy in the Library was no mere excuse: in

1963 we had to prepare two Russian operas, Mussorgsky's "Khovanschina" and "Katerina Ismailova" by Shostakovitch. "Khovanschina" was to be done in the Shostakovitch version and the score came from the Soviet Union on microfilm and had to be printed and enlarged. The bulky, thick photographic paper meant that we needed several volumes for each act. We had three months to prepare all the parts and I became positively organized with a chart on the wall showing which of my army of extra copyists had which bit and how much had been completed. It was to be sung in English but the days of endless word writing were long gone, we made one vocal score and then photographed it as soon as we had the translation made by Edward Downes. And then the Rumanian conductor, Silvestri, said he must have the English translation in his full score as well; it was very difficult to write on the glossy photographic paper and Diana finally managed to make it show up clearly by writing in red ink. "Katerina Ismailova" was even more hectic, we had exactly one month and only one printed full score. Fortunately xeroxing had just become available and we were able to make ten copies in sections to be distributed to the copyists; and after all our frantic work the parts arrived from Russia the day before the first orchestra rehearsal! They were full of mistakes so we never used them.

A far more massive piece of work was to fall to my lot when, in 1966, it was decided to attempt the recreation of Berlioz' original 1838 version of his opera "Benvenuto Cellini", following the lead given by Arthur Hammond in a Carl Rosa production of 1957. I believe the Covent Garden venture was largely at the instigation of Maurits Sillem, a member of the music staff and a great Berlioz enthusiast. The only published score was of a version made by Berlioz some fourteen years after the first performance, for use by Liszt when he decided to put on the opera at Weimar. Now a complete edition of Berlioz was being contemplated by Bärenreiter, the publishers, and the general editor, Hugh Macdonald, went to the Paris Opera, where nothing is ever thrown away, to do a great deal of detective work among the old orchestral parts of the first performance of "Cellini". A stream of photostats and manuscript pages of score which he had compiled himself from the scraps of material that he had found, began to reach me and for nine months I worked day and night to construct the new full score.

Photographic negatives were prepared of everything: whole,

unaltered pages of the published version interspersed with sections that I had copied and dozens more pages containing countless amendments, including the greater part of the last act. Even the words as well as the music had to be changed at times – for example, Liszt had not approved of the Pope being presented as a character in an opera and the role had been given to a Cardinal; now His Holiness was to have his part back. I did manage to lessen the work-load by borrowing the negatives of the orchestral parts from the BBC so we could amend and add rather than copy out an entire part – although quite often it was quicker to do the latter. A piano reduction had also to be made (mostly by Tim Killar) for the new vocal scores.

The opera was to be conducted by John Pritchard who belonged to the school of maestri who like to have their ideas on dynamics fixed in writing in the parts in the fond hope that the players will then pay more attention to them. When rehearsals were under way the parts for the large orchestra of 90 or so players would be spread out all round the Library after each session and Jane Gore and I would await with dread the arrival of Maurits Sillem with the day's alterations. He would produce these from his pocket, neatly transcribed on the back of a cigarette packet which he apparently found more convenient than a notepad. He then left us to it and we spent the rest of the day progressing slowly round the endless piles, putting in all the marks which we might well have to take out again next day!

Under Pritchard the opera was musically very exciting, especially a romance for Cellini in the "Mardi Gras" scene (the only aria from the later version not in the original) the great chorus of the metal-workers – *les ciseleurs* – and an aria for the *travesti* role of Ascanio most exquisitely sung by Yvonne Minton. Dramatically the story line was still clumsy and particularly unconvincing in the second half, in no way worthy of such an inspired score.

It had been a monumental task but, although I am not generally in favour of returning to original versions, so often a composer's second thoughts are better, I felt that in the case of "Benvenuto Cellini" it was worth doing. For once, also, the work of the Library received an acknowledgement in the programme which encouraged me. After this there would be no more great operatic deadlines for us to meet; it would be new versions of "Sleeping Beauty" all the way for the next eighteen years – or that is what it felt like!

172

· 33 ·

THERE is no doubt that one can become positively addicted to reminiscing but I know that the moment has arrived when I must write the epilogue to these recollections, in view of the title I have given them. However busy we might be in the Library I had gradually to face the fact that a stage in my life was over and that when I expressed an opinion it would no longer come as a voice from the pit but increasingly as a voice from the past. Now when music was made I would no longer be involved in its making but hear it as an ordinary, well-informed member of the audience. The evening sessions in the "Nag's Head" or the "King's Arms", talking shop during the interval or after a show that finished early, were gone for good. I gave up frequenting the Canteen as a tendency to corpulence had obliged me to restrict myself to midday snacks of the lettuce and Ryvita variety, supplied from home and eaten at my desk and I suppose that in this way I became somewhat of a recluse.

I also became a trifle curmudgeonly on the subject of the new generation of conductors who found it necessary to cover beautiful clean scores that were not their own with frantic and often indelible pencil reminders which we could not remove without removing the print as well and which made it impossible to offer the score to anyone else. None of my giants needed more than the score as it stood and I remembered Kempe's mildly reproachful: "There's a mark in my score of 'Götterdämmerung', Mr. Savage. Please take it out." I even went so far as to ask a young conductor fiercely whether he did not know the music if he needed so many helpful signs and remarks. I rather think he said he didn't have the time – but he bought his own scores after that. On the whole, though, I was contented and suffered no psychomatic symptoms, depression or even intense feelings of regret – the moment had come when I must stop playing and I was able to accept it. At first, certainly, I felt rather strange; I was not a man of hobbies, music having always absorbed me entirely, and so I spent a great deal of time at home in the evenings sitting in my chair doing nothing in particular. My eldest daughter, Imogen, sounded the alarm with more affectionate concern than respect: "Something must be done – the Old Man is turning into a gonk!" So I eventually found myself for a short time the Chairman of the local Music Club, a long-established institution which was going through a patch of financial low water. Committees are not at all my scene and my spell as Chairman did little to improve the situation, apart from one very profitable evening when I arranged for "Ballet for All" to perform for us. I am glad to say that when I resigned the Club fell into extremely capable hands and is now probably one of the best-run and most successful in the country, so I did not do it any lasting harm. I had also brought me into contact with local musical talent and at last I began to grasp the baton that had tempted me for so many years.

I knew that I had finally found the only hobby that would satisfy me; to start with it would be simply a Mozart Divertimento for a Members' Concert of the Music Club or a group to accompany a local organist who wanted to do a Handel concerto, but in 1971 I had enough contacts to form an amateur chamber orchestra, meeting not for the usual pedestrian weekly session but for short and very intensive rehearsal periods two or three times a year before a concert; and as I write we have recently given our thirty-second. In the first years we were greatly helped by fine young string players from Pamela Spofforth's "Pro Corda" whom she sent to gain orchestral experience; now we can call on the astonishingly gifted pupils of the Yehudi Menuhin School as our soloists. It is written in the constitution of the society that every programme must contain a work by Mozart but I am thankful to say that administrative matters have been taken over by kind and practical friends, leaving me free to enjoy myself. I admit that I still find it hard to accept the attitudes and even the limitations of amateur players and am a hard task-master. I also tell them frequent stories of conductors who died before the younger members were born, but with the memory of those great men always fresh in my mind I strive to make my orchestra play, as a friend put it paradoxically but aptly "better than they can," and this seems to me a fitting way to round off the life of a practical musician.

November 1984

INDEX

Aida (Verdi) 56, 123, 129, 142, 144–146
Ainsworth, Robert 54
Alexandra, George & Jack 26, 53, 66
Ansermet, Ernest 38, 99
Aprahamian, Felix 67
Ashton, Sir Frederick 132, 133, 161, 164
Augarde, Edward 24–26

Baines, Anthony 9, 48, 103, 104
Ballet Companies (*various*) 110, 111, 132, 134, 135, 174
Beard, Paul 41, 46
Beecham, Sir Thomas 10, 11, 20, 23–25, 30, 38, 40, 42–45, 48–50, 52, 55–59, 61, 62, 67–71, 88, 91, 94, 95, 100, 102, 128, 136–138, 159
Beer, Sydney 42, 66, 87
Benvenuto Cellini (Berlioz) 88, 138, 171, 172
Berlin Philharmonic Orchestra 45, 53
Billy Budd (Britten) 138, 139
Bohème, La (Puccini) 32
Boris Godunov (Mussorgsky) 121, 122, 138
Borsdorf, Adolf 9, 29, 84, 101
Boult, Sir Adrian 42, 71, 72, 83, 90, 94, 109, 118
Bradley, Francis 66, 92
Brahms, Johannes 68
Brain family 9, 16, 17
Braithwaite, Warwick 95, 124
Bree, Bernard 134
Britten, Benjamin 21, 40, 98, 138, 139, 142, 159
Brook, Peter 122, 123
Brunskill, Muriel 54, 125

Callas, Maria 121, 141, 142, 158, 159
Cameron, Basil 60, 61, 71, 72, 83, 91, 95
Clark, Ralph 13
Coates, Albert 35, 36, 99
Coates, Edith 114, 140
Coliseum 27–29
Collingwood, Laurence 52
Cruft, Eugene & John 15, 59
Cundell, Edric 18, 95

Dali, Salvador 113

De Basil Ballets 47, 48
Del Mar, Norman 137
De Valois, Dame Ninette 162
Dent, Professor E. J. 113, 114
Don Carlos (Verdi) 150, 155
Don Giovanni (Mozart) 60, 110, 123, 130
Douglas, Roy 167
Downes, Edward 138, 150
Draper, Charles 9, 20

Edinburgh, Duke of 142, 160
Elgar, Sir Edward 46, 56, 72, 85, 88
Elizabeth II, H.M. Queen 159, 160
Evans, Edgar 119, 123, 129, 130

Façade (Walton) 97, 98
Fairy Queen (Purcell) 113
Feasey, Norman 59, 60, 110, 113, 116
Fenby, Eric 23, 55
Festivals 10, 40, 41, 159
Fielding, Harold 83, 84
Film Sessions 29, 55, 98
Fistoulari, Anatole 93–95
Flagstad, Kirsten 44, 53, 121, 137
Fonteyn, Dame Margot 113, 132, 163
Furtwängler, Wilhelm 45, 53, 54, 170

Gardner, John 61, 110, 114
Geissmar, Dr. Berta 49, 56, 57, 59, 67, 100, 101, 159
Gellhorn, Peter 110, 117, 123, 138, 143
George VI, H.M. King 38, 68
German Tour 49–51
Giulini, Carlo Maria 11, 155, 156
Gloriana (Britten) 142, 144
Glynne, Howell 140
Gobbi, Tito 153, 155
Goodall, Sir Reginald 116, 117, 124
Goossens, Sir Eugene 9, 55
Goossens, Leon 9, 28, 31, 41, 50, 66
Goossens, Marie 9, 25, 26, 60
Gregory, Charles 66, 68, 82, 92, 104
Grieg Piano Concerto 72, 86, 88

Hambourg, Charles 71, 95
Hammond, Arthur 171
Harewood, Earl of 159, 170
Harty, Sir Hamilton 38, 39
Hawkes, Ralph 68, 81
Helpmann, Robert 110
Hylton, Jack 82, 83, 91

Irving, K. Ernest 29, 98
Irving, Robert 128, 134, 135, 162

Jacob, Dr. Gordon 21, 133, 134
Johnston, Maurice 33, 55
Joyce, Eileen 72, 82

Kempe, Rudolf 11, 23, 147–149, 151, 154, 155, 173
Kerry, Muriel 111, 159, 167
Killar, Tim 127, 133, 137, 172
Kleiber, Carlos 59
Kleiber, Erich 11, 45, 50, 58, 59, 71, 124, 128–130, 139, 140, 147, 148, 150, 170
Klemperer, Otto 161
Knappertsbusch, Hans 52, 53
Koanga (Delius) 36, 37
Konwit schny, Franz 160
Krauss, Clemens 11, 128, 130, 131
Kreisler, Fritz 42, 45
Kubelik, Rafael 81, 115, 151, 153, 154

Lambert, Constant 23, 52, 69, 95, 98, 113, 117, 133
Lanchbery, John 128, 133, 161, 162, 167
Lanigan, John 138, 154, 169
Laurence, Frederick 25, 26, 36, 43, 55, 61, 65, 110
Lehmann, Lotte 30, 59
Leider, Frieda 30
Lewkowitch, Jason 24
Liddell, Alvar 13
Lohengrin (Wagner) 30–32, 125, 161
Lowe, Fred 163, 169, 170

Madam Butterfly (Puccini) 149
Mann, William 161, 162, 167
Manon (Massenet) 115, 116
Matthews, Thomas 56, 91, 141

175

McColl, Anthony 166
*Meistersinger von Nürnberg,
Die* (Wagner) 44, 45, 116,
131, 136, 155
Melchior, Lauritz 30
Menges, Herbert 27
Middle East Ballet Tour
163–166
Midgley, Walter 117, 124,
125, 130
Moor, Charles 30, 36, 60, 62,
122
Moore, Grace 32
Morley, Reginald 66
Münch, Charles 23, 99, 102

National Anthems 56, 146,
159, 165, 166
New World Symphony
(Dvorak) 72

Old Vic. 26, 27
Olympians, The (Bliss) 125
Orchestral Porters 71, 145,
159
Otcharkoff, Theodore 13
Otello (Verdi) 153

Parry, Hilda (*1st wife of
R.T.S.*) 14, 35, 62, 65, 92,
104
Parsifal (Wagner) 61
Pears, Sir Peter 22, 23, 87, 98,
151, 152
Peter Grimes (Britten) 94,
102, 123
Pierrot Lunaire (Schoenberg)
97, 98
Piper, John 139
Plumley, Roy 21
Potts, Dr Denys 96
Pougnet, Jean 91, 95
Poulenc, Francis 155
Priestley, J. B. 72, 125
Prince Igor (Borodin) 33
Pritchard, Sir John 141, 152,
155, 172
Promenade Concerts 14, 15,
91, 92
Pryce-Jones, Alan 114

Queen of Spades
(Tschaikowsky) 128, 129
Queen's Hall 17, 41, 42, 46,
68, 72, 85

Rachmaninoff, Serge 41
Rankl, Karl 95, 104, 105,
113–117, 123–125, 130,
131, 137, 147, 148, 170
Raybould, Clarence 35
Read, Ernest 17
Read Senior Orchestra 17, 19,
22, 35

Recording Sessions 37–39, 69
Reiner, Fritz 45
Rendall, Frank 34, 92
Repetiteurs 60–62, 110, 115,
154
Rescigno, Antonio 158, 159
Rhodesian Season 142–146
Rignold, Hugo 91, 128
Rigoletto (Verdi) 119, 130
Ring, The (Wagner) 35, 44,
45, 53, 54, 121, 148, 151,
156, 160, 168
Robinson, Stanford 52
Rosenkavalier, Der
(R. Strauss) 15, 36, 50, 58, 59,
124, 128, 140
Roth, Ernst 97
Royal Ballet Company 128,
132–134
Royal College of Music
18–23
Royal Opera Chorus 110,
113, 122, 154
Royal Opera House Library
(*work of*) 105, 110–114,
121, 122, 125, 127–129,
133–135, 152, 154, 158,
159, 161, 167–169, 171,
172
Royal Opera House
Orchestra 16, 119–120,
128, 131, 155, 159
Russell, Thomas 66–70, 84,
85, 90, 99, 100, 105

Salome (R. Strauss) 52, 53,
95, 123, 148
Sargent, Sir Malcolm 26, 46,
47, 71, 72, 82, 85, 88, 90,
94, 151, 152, 167, 168
Savage, Elizabeth (*mother*)
12, 15, 17, 62, 92
Savage, Ernest (*father*) 12–14,
17, 22, 62, 92, 118, 157
Savage (*family*) 12, 65, 83,
119, 124, 126, 128, 145,
146, 157
Savage, R. Temple
(*orchestrations,
arrangements, etc*) 42, 81,
87, 93, 113, 134, 146, 165,
168
Savage, Valerie (*wife*) 9, 21,
23, 103–106, 112,
117–119, 126, 139, 142,
160
Shadwick, Joseph 110, 112,
119, 122, 141
Shaw, George Bernard 27
Shostakovitch, Dmitry 138
Sillem, Maurits 171, 172
Simpson, Dudley 163, 165,
166
Slobodskaya, Oda 36

Smith, Morris 27, 135, 136,
143, 144, 170
Solti, Sir Georg 121, 127, 155,
163, 168, 169
Stage Bands 56, 122, 123,
149, 154, 160
Stead, Frank 66, 110, 142,
143
Stein, Erwin 97, 98
Stiedry, Fritz 148
Strauss, Richard 42
Street, Aileen 21, 22, 34, 92,
105, 106
Supervía, Conchita 32, 33
Sutherland, Dame Joan 160
Sylvia (Delibes) 134

Tannhaüser (Wagner) 26, 149
Tauber, Richard 59, 62, 95,
96
Tausky, Vilem 93, 141
Taylor, Charles 141, 152
Tertis, Lionel 55, 56
Thurston, Frederick 20, 24,
25
Tippett, Sir Michael 152, 153
Tooley, Sir John 151, 163,
168, 169, 170
Traviata, La (Verdi) 60, 116,
122
Tristan und Isolde (Wagner)
18, 30, 45, 61, 124, 131,
155
Troilus & Cressida (Walton)
151, 152
Trojans, The (Berlioz) 154,
155
Turner, Dame Eva 56, 117

*Under the Spreading Chestnut
Tree* (Weinberger) 68

Vaughan-Williams, Ralph 40,
42, 46, 47, 136
Village Romeo & Juliet
(Delius) 23, 25, 35, 137
Visconti, Lucchino 150, 155

Walter, Bruno 15, 26, 96
Walton, Sir William 81, 89,
98, 99, 142, 151, 152
Ward, Alan 13
Webster, Sir David 105, 123,
128, 135, 141, 143, 146,
158, 160
Weingartner, Felix von 11,
16, 47, 62, 69
Wood, Sir Henry 14, 15, 41,
91, 97
Wozzeck (Berg) 42, 139, 140
Wright, Olive 134, 147

Zefferelli, Franco 127, 150,
160